For the two women in my life who continue to inspire me:

My mother,

who taught me lessons I follow to this day.

And my daughter,

who motivated me to pursue my passion.

Marwa ♡ مروة

sahten

A SPIRITED CELEBRATION OF MODERN MIDDLE EASTERN FOOD

Yallateef!

MARWA MAKOOL

PHOTOGRAPHY & STYLING: DEAN CAMBRAY

FOREWORD: BOB HART

oasisbakery.com.au

HARTBEAT MEDIA

FOREWORD

Many joyful Lebanese expressions are inspired by the idea of food: the taste of it, the sharing of it, the preparation of it and an unconditional love of it.

One of these expressions is *yallateef* – often an exclamation of delight but also, in Marwa Makool's flamboyant and delectable world of Middle Eastern cuisine, the name of a specific creation.

And *yallateef*, coincidentally, is a creation which, like so much of Marwa's food, is inclined to provoke exclamations of delight from those encountering it for the first time: *Wow! Crikey! Yallateef!!!*

Another such expression is *t'fadalou* which translates, loosely, as a respectful invitation to table – something routinely issued in Lebanese society where the sharing of food, and lots of it, ideally with guests, expected or otherwise, is a pillar of living a good and fulfilling life.

And it would be hard to imagine a life lived better than that lived by Marwa Makool, who almost dances her way through what many would regard as the intolerable pressures of running a frantic kitchen in one of Melbourne's busiest and best-loved food outlets – her family's incomparable, all-things-to-all-appetites food empire: the Oasis Bakery.

Now it's hard to explain Oasis to anyone who has never been there. For one thing, it is vast: an Aladdin's cave of spices, herbs, Middle Eastern delicacies and culinary exotica from all corners of the world rubbing shoulders with everyday essentials.

And for another, it is seductive: you may begin with an empty shopping trolley and a short list of requirements. But you will leave with mountains of "essentials" you had never quite regarded as essential until you found them on the groaning shelves of Oasis. *Yallateef!*

If you choose to arrive at Oasis hungry, then you choose wisely. The food aromas rising from the bustling kitchen behind the insanely busy cafeteria are hypnotic – the stuff of which dreams are made. And you will soon be indulging, intemperately I trust, in Oasis food, rather than simply dreaming about it.

Because all of this food is masterminded by Marwa Makool – an instinctive, passionate, innovative and creative cook.

The world is not her oyster. The world is her baba ghanoush, hummous, shanklish, tabouli, fatteh, labneh and all the rest. Her world is one of ancient and glorious foodstuffs – redolent of mysticism and tradition and holylands and romance.

This is the food of the Levant. Re-interpreted and made seductively accessible by a remarkable and irrepressible woman of the Levant who is now a culinary force to be reckoned with in her Australian community.

This woman is an original: she is innovative and industrious beyond all reason. In fact, Marwa Makool is a woman with whom, I can promise, you are about to fall in love.

– Bob Hart

YALLATEEF... *the wow factor*

Peel and quarter a large onion and coarsely chop it in a food processor.

Add two peeled cloves of garlic, ¼ bunch of rinsed parsley, ¼ bunch of rinsed coriander, 100g unsalted cashew pieces, 100g raw pistachio kernels, ½ cup EV olive oil, pulsing after each addition.

Add the spices and seasoning: ½ tsp sea salt, ½ tsp sweet paprika, ½ tsp dried mint, ½ tsp crushed black pepper, ½ tsp Aleppo pepper, ½ tsp chermoula mix, ¼ tsp chilli powder. Pulse until it becomes a chunky paste and store, topped with a layer of rice bran oil. Yallateef will keep, refrigerated, for up to two months in an air-tight container. Add more rice bran oil if it begins to dry out.

Labneh: recipe, page 15.

Contents

🌴 Denotes ingredients available only at Oasis.

INTRODUCTION

Marwa Makool is a chef. She is also an original thinker, a rule-breaker, a culinary evangelist and… an enchantress.

Her food is just that: *her* food. It is Middle Eastern, certainly. But she has revisited, lightened and simplified an entire food tradition – respectfully, but fearlessly.

Food has been a lifelong obsession, but not one that was encouraged during her childhood in Lebanon where her mother became her unwitting inspiration.

"I loved to watch her cook, but I had to do so from a distance as she would not let me work in her kitchen," says Marwa.

"She believed it was hard and unattractive work, and she wanted me to be a princess – never to have to work hard, ever, in my life.

"Her dream was that I would be well educated and sit in an office, perhaps as a lawyer. And I tried. I studied law, briefly. But it was not for me.

"As a small girl, I would watch my mother work with the few spices she had in her pantry.

"And when I was at home on my own, I would go into the kitchen and remix and re-label them. She never knew. But my father noticed that the flavour of our food, often, was different.

"If his comments were favourable, I would continue with that spice mix. And if they were not, it was back to the drawing board. Nobody knew what I was up to."

Marwa's childhood experiments took place in her home town of Karem Asfour, in the Akkar region, at a time when the country was engulfed in civil war. And yet, her childhood was idyllic.

"My mother always found a way to do the things that had to be done," says Marwa. "She taught me how to approach life. She taught me to smile, and always to be content with what I had.

"She ensured that my childhood was happy and carefree and delicious. And in this way, she shaped my life and my food: because of her, my food is happy food.

"Some people, when they are stressed, do yoga or go dancing. But when I am stressed, I go to my kitchen and create.

"My food does not fit into any category: it's my food. Take a classic dish like ejjeh which, traditionally, is made with flour, a bit of parsley and eggs. And it is cooked flat in a lot of oil.

"But I introduced vegetables, and I like it fluffy and light, and I added labneh. When my Lebanese customers tasted it, they knew it was ejjeh, but they also knew it was different. Fortunately, they loved it."

Marwa left Lebanon in 1986 and came to Melbourne where her first child, Natalie, was born. Two sons, George and Michael, followed and, by the time she was 25, Marwa Makool had three children and a family food business to juggle.

And while she juggled, she cooked. And cooked. And then… she caught her breath, and cooked some more.

"I love Lebanese food," says Marwa.

"But there is a Lebanese tradition that involves eating until you feel unable to move. I have never liked that and yet, I love to eat.

"So I have addressed it. My food is Middle Eastern, but with a twist: you can eat a lot of it without ever feeling heavy, and without discovering, suddenly, that you can't move."

How does she do that? *Yallateef!* It's magic. Marwa's magic. Woven around secrets she shares in this remarkable collection of her unique recipes.

TAHINI DIP... *a silken staple*

This flavoursome and nutritious dip is often served with fish or vegetables, and as a complement to falafel. I cook several dishes in tahini – among them samkee harra (spicy fish fillets, Page 135) and kafta in tahini (Page 111). Tahini dip is easy to execute, and an essential dish to master.

INGREDIENTS

1 cup tahini paste

½ tsp salt

2 cloves garlic

½ cup lemon juice

METHOD

• Place the garlic cloves and salt in a food processor and pulse until smooth.

• Add the tahini, 1½ cups of water and lemon juice to the garlic paste and pulse until you achieve a silky-smooth consistency.

NOTE: Tahini dip can be placed in a sterilised jar and stored in the fridge where it will keep for up to two weeks. Chopped, flat-leaf parsley can be added, but not if you intend to keep the dip: add only to the portion you are about to use.

HUMMOUS... *the stuff of life*

Legal challenges between Middle Eastern nations over the origin of hummous are hardly surprising: in Lebanon, where the dish originated, this is a food around which life revolves. It combines many of the ingredients around which our cuisine revolves, also: chickpeas, tahini, garlic and lemon juice. Olive oil makes an appearance as – in my presentation – does Maras chilli.

INGREDIENTS

60g dried chickpeas (medium sized)

1 tsp tahini

1 tsp lemon juice

pinch sea salt

½ tsp crushed garlic

EV olive oil (to serve)

Maras chilli (to serve)

METHOD

• Soak chickpeas overnight; drain, wash and simmer in fresh water for 30-40 minutes, or until tender.

• Rinse thoroughly.

• Place the cooked chickpeas, tahini, lemon juice, garlic and salt in a food processer and process until a smooth paste is formed.

• Serve with a drizzle of EV olive oil and a sprinkle of Maras chilli.

NOTE: Tinned chickpeas can substituted for the cooked chickpeas: use 250g of the drained and rinsed contents of a tin.

FALAFEL… *making vegetarianism fun*

This wondrous food originates from Egypt, but was accepted with wild enthusiasm from the moment it was introduced, as a street food, into Lebanon. The way Australians have accepted it, also, mirrors that level of enthusiasm, and why would it not? It is delicious with lots of golden, nutty crunch from being deep-fried. But it is also vegetarian and wholesome, indicating it ticks a surprising range of boxes. In addition to which, falafel allows plenty of self-expression in terms of the things you can combine with it in a wrap.

INGREDIENTS

250g dried (medium) chickpeas

100g split, dried fava beans

1 onion

1 clove garlic

1 bunch parsley

½ bunch coriander

½ tsp cumin

½ tsp salt

½ tsp pepper

1 tsp falafel spices 🌴

½ tsp bicarbonate soda

METHOD

• Soak the chickpeas and the beans overnight.

• Drain and rinse them just before use.

• Chop all ingredients (excluding the bicarb) in a food processor.

• In a large bowl, add the bicarb to the mixture and combine well. Leave to set into a paste for a few minutes.

• Place some paste on top of a falafel machine (ol'eb felalfer – illustrated) while holding down the lever, and remove excess paste (which can be returned to the mixture).

• Release the lever, allowing the formed pattie to fall from the machine. Deep fry the patties in batches in very hot oil (180 C). Rice bran or any other nut (peanut) or seed (canola) oil with which you are comfortable can be used in a large pot or, better still, a deep fryer – until golden brown. Drain on absorbent kitchen paper.

• Serve the cooked patties with tahini dip (Page 12) – on their own, with salad, or in wraps.

HUMMOUS AWARMA...*added magic*

This modest dish manages to take a simple, nutritious dip to another level. There is something poetic about the affinity the versatile hummous has with simply cooked lamb. My father-in-law, in fact, is so passionate about this dish that he assumes, usually correctly, I will prepare it for him whenever he visits. Whereupon he eats it, lovingly and meditatively, with pita bread.

INGREDIENTS

200g lean, premium cut lamb, diced (fillets or backstraps work well)

1 small onion, diced

1 tsp rice bran oil

¼ tsp sea salt

¼ tsp mixed spice (baharat) 🌿

¼ tsp dried mint

50g pine nuts

300g hummous

METHOD

• Heat the oil in a medium/hot pan and add the onion. Sauté until it begins to colour, and then add the lamb, all at once.

• Add the salt, spices, mint and pine nuts and cook, moving in the pan to sear the lamb evenly, for about 3 minutes, or until cooked to your satisfaction.

• Spread a thin, even layer of hummous on a flat plate and top with the sizzling lamb mixture.

LABNEH... *a cultured revelation*

Labneh is a necessary and reassuring creation in any Lebanese kitchen and, like so many of the dishes around which our cuisine revolves, is deliciously simple to make, even if you choose to make your own yoghurt, as I do.

INGREDIENTS

1 litre whole milk

2 tbs natural yoghurt

salt

sunflower oil

zaatar

METHOD

• In a saucepan, bring the milk gently to the boil. Remove from the heat and allow to cool to body warmth, or until you can easily tolerate it to the touch.

• Stir the yoghurt into half a cup of the warm milk, allowing it to dissolve fully, and then add to the rest of the milk and stir well.

• Cover the mixture and leave to stand in a warm place for 24 hours.

• Place a clean, thin tea towel or – better still – muslin (or layered cheesecloth) in a large strainer. Salt the yoghurt mixture to taste and pour into the strainer over a bowl.

• Tie the material at the top to enclose the yoghurt mixture, but leave it in the strainer in a bowl and keep it in the fridge for 12 hours, or until the desired texture is achieved, discarding the liquid that drips into the bowl. (Alternatively, you can hang the wrapped yoghurt over a bowl, but few fridges will easily accommodate that technique. Also, remember that extra time means a firmer texture.)

• To serve, spread the labneh (Picture: Page 6) in a bowl or on a plate, sprinkle with zaatar and drizzle with sunflower oil.

• For a lively variation, once you have prepared your labneh, but before you serve it, prepare this alternative dish:

• Wearing a pair of disposable gloves, dip your fingers into olive oil and roll the labneh into small balls.

• Place these in a container with sunflower oil and, for a bit of added excitement, add dried chilli flakes to the oil.

NOTE: These lively and addictive labneh balls will keep in oil for up to 3 months, but I suspect you will have eaten them long before then.

FOUL MUDAMMAS... *far from foolish*

This simple and gloriously sustaining dish of Egyptian extraction – it is a dish the Pharaohs almost certainly consumed, not to mention their pyramid-building labour force – will power you through the day and, indeed, makes a fine breakfast. It is both vegetarian and vegan, but its culinary appeal is universal and its nutritional value significant. "Foul" is the Arabic word for fava beans. In Egypt it is generally made without chickpeas and often served with hard-boiled eggs. But try it, instead, with poached eggs on top.

INGREDIENTS

500g dried fava beans

200g dried medium chickpeas

2 cloves crushed garlic

2 tbs EV olive oil

1 tsp sea salt

2 tbs lemon juice

½ tsp mixed spice (baharat) 🕷

pinch dried mint

parsley to garnish

METHOD

• Soak the fava beans and chickpeas separately overnight.

• Drain and rinse both.

• Place the fava beans in a saucepan and cover with 2.5 litres of water. Bring to a boil and simmer, covered, for 90 minutes.

• Add the chickpeas to the fava beans, return to a boil and simmer, covered, for 30 minutes.

• Combine salt, crushed garlic, mixed spice and lemon juice as a dressing.

• Drain the chickpeas and fava beans, reserving a cup of the cooking liquid. Add this to the dressing. If there is insufficient liquid left to do this, use plain boiling water.

• Add the finished dressing to the mixed beans, combine well, and serve with olive oil and fresh parsley.

EMTABLEH... *the yoghurt drink of champions*

This ancient and refreshing yoghurt drink was once regarded as the hero of summer. That was in an era when salad was not on anyone's radar. Instead, this wonderful concoction was kept in large terracotta pots and served as a light and nutritious lunch. It remains a favourite of mine when the weather warms up: I make vast quantities and share it among the family.

INGREDIENTS

250g pearl barley

100g dried chickpeas

1kg natural yoghurt

1 tbs sea salt

METHOD

• Soak the barley and chickpeas overnight. Rinse and drain them.

• Bring them to a boil in a large saucepan in 3 litres of water and simmer for 90 minutes, stirring regularly. Remove from the heat and leave in the water to cool.

• Mix the yoghurt with ½ litre of water and add the salt.

• Add this mixture to the barley, chickpeas and the water in which they have cooled.

• Chill, and serve cold – either in a large cup or a small bowl.

TZATZIKI... *a gift from the Greeks*

This refreshingly simple dip of Greek or Turkish origin can accompany, and will enhance, hot or cold dishes – including stuffed vine leaves, kebbeh, grilled lamb or even traditional rice (Page 78). It is a fixture on any self-respecting mezza table.

INGREDIENTS

2 cups thick, natural yoghurt

2 large or 6 Lebanese cucumbers

2 tsp dried dill or 3 tsp fresh dill tips

6 fresh mint leaves

1 tsp crushed garlic

pinch sea salt

METHOD

• Shred or grate the unpeeled cucumbers and chop the mint leaves, finely in both cases.

• Add the cucumbers, dill, garlic, mint and salt to the yoghurt. Mix thoroughly.

• Check the salt level, adding more as required, and serve the dish as a pleasing embellishment to just about anything.

BABA GHANOUSH… *a labour of love*

Baba ghanoush translates as "spoiled father" because of the work involved in preparing it. The suggestion is that husbands and fathers are indeed spoiled, and fortunate, to have someone willing to make this opulent dip for them. Quite so!

INGREDIENTS

1 large firm, dark eggplant

1 clove garlic

pinch sea salt

1 tsp lemon juice

2 tbs tahini paste

EV olive oil

METHOD

• Roast the eggplant by placing it over a flame on a gas stove top, turning carefully with tongs as it blackens and softens. The eggplant also can be oven roasted or even roasted in a small pan on the stove, but blackening over a flame delivers the characteristic smoky flavour.

• Carefully peel the blackened eggplant, ensuring no skin remains as it will make your dip less attractive.

• In a food processor, combine the garlic and salt, pulse until fine, and then add the lemon juice and tahini. Pulse. Finally, add the roughly chopped eggplant and process until the desired texture is achieved. This dip should be smooth, but a measure of texture is acceptable.

• Serve with a drizzle of EV olive oil.

NOTE: If you place the blackened eggplant in a large bowl and cover, while it begins to cool, with plastic cling film, you will find it easier to peel.

HALOUMI & MUSHROOM…*celebrating differences*

There is an improbable range of textures at play in this dish. Also, there is quite an array of flavours – all of which, curiously, combine harmoniously. This dish, in fact, makes a superb hot breakfast if you are seeking an alternative to eggs. But remember: grilled haloumi must be eaten hot if you plan to wallow in that seductive softness.

INGREDIENTS

300g mixed salad leaves, washed

½ tsp rice bran oil

100g sliced mushrooms

50g washed baby spinach

50g Archie's blend 2 🐾

300g haloumi cheese, cut into 5mm slices

½ tsp Maras chilli

½ tsp crushed black pepper

METHOD

• Heat the oil in a trustworthy pan and add the mushrooms; cook briskly for 3 minutes.

• Add the Archie's blend and the spices to the mushrooms. Stir for about a minute.

• Add the spinach, and toss everything together so the spinach wilts. Remove from the heat.

• Meanwhile, heat a second pan and in it grill the haloumi for two minutes on each side.

• Time your operations so both elements of the meal are ready at the same time and can be served, hot, together – the haloumi on top of the mixed salad leaves and the mushroom mixture to the side.

SHANKLISH... *a cheesy aristocrat*

This wondrous yoghurt cheese is not a creation as widely known in Australia as, say, hummous or baba ghanoush. But its reputation is growing and, given time, and a bit of understanding, it is certain to soar in the popularity stakes.

INGREDIENTS

2kg natural yoghurt

1 tbs salt

100g dried thyme

METHOD

• In a non-reactive saucepan, combine the yoghurt and 1 litre water over medium heat.

• Continue to heat the mixture until the edges are beginning to boil, and then take off the heat and set aside for six hours.

• Pour mixture into a strainer lined with cheese-cloth or muslin and suspend, overnight, over a bowl. Tie the cloth to shape the cheese. You can even use a clean pillowcase for this process.

• You can also, if you like, weight the bag to force out more of the liquid.

• Place the mixture in a bowl and work in the salt with your fingers. Spend about three minutes doing this.

• For spicy shanklish, at this point add chilli flakes to the mixture.

• Form the mixture into large balls, pressing them firmly to ensure they will hold together, and then roll each in the thyme, making sure the entire ball is covered.

• Leave in the fridge for 2 days to give the cheese more time to dry out and set before eating it, ideally with olive oil.

NOTE: To make aged shanklish, simply place the balls, before you roll them in thyme, on absorbent kitchen towels on a tray. Rest them in a cool, dry place for as much as two or three months – the first two or three days of that time in the sun. At the end of the total rest period, you will find a thin layer of mould has formed. Carefully remove this with a knife and roll the cheese in dried thyme. Keep the aged shanklish covered, and in the refrigerator: you will find it has a bold and interesting flavour – rather like blue cheese.

EJJEH...*golden discs of wonder*

This recipe is my own, expanded version of the basic dish – traditionally made with just egg and parsley. My recipe adds more vegetables and spices, giving the dish a new range of flavours and textures. Ejjeh is usually fried, but it also can be baked in an oiled baking dish. This process will take just 10 minutes at 180 C. Fried ejjeh, however, is generally preferred. These crunchy rissoles can be eaten as they are, or used as wrap fillings.

INGREDIENTS

2 carrots, grated

1 zucchini, grated

¼ small pumpkin, peeled and grated

½ onion, grated

1 small red capsicum, seeded and grated

½ bunch flat-leaf parsley, chopped

1 tbs garlic & herbs 🌴

1 tsp dried mint

1 tsp mixed spice (baharat) 🌴

1 tsp Aleppo pepper

1 tsp fine black pepper

1 tsp sea salt

2 cups SR flour

3 eggs

rice bran oil (to fry in)

garnish

labneh, pine nuts, parsley, olives

METHOD

• Place the carrots, zucchini, pumpkin, onion and capsicum in a large bowl with the parsley.

• Beat the eggs and add to the vegetables. Combine the flour with 2 cups water and add this, also, to the mixture.

• Add the spices to the mixture, and mix well to form a dough.

• Fill a deep saucepan or a deep-fryer with rice bran oil and heat to at least 170 C.

• Using a large spoon, drop dollops of the mixture into the hot oil in several batches so as not to lower the temperature of the oil.

• Once they are golden on the underside, flip them over until both sides are a deep golden colour. Lift them from the oil and place on paper towels to drain.

• To garnish ejjeh, place a spoonful of labneh on top and finish with an olive, pine nuts and parsley.

BREAKFAST TAJINE... *the perfect start*

This glorious creation is served – at breakfast time, obviously – in the Oasis Bakery. But if you can't find your way to Murrumbeena at first light, you can always make it for yourself – ideally in a small tajine which you can buy, at any time of day, at Oasis.

Before starting on the dish, ensure your new tajine is seasoned by soaking the top and the base in water overnight, sun-drying them thoroughly and then coating them lightly with vegetable oil. Bake the oil into the tajine by placing in a 100 C oven for an hour. And that's it. You will only ever need to do this once.

INGREDIENTS

1 large brown onion, chopped

2 tbs rice bran oil

800g minced lamb

sea salt

freshly ground black pepper

3 tomatoes, roughly chopped

100g pine nuts

Maras chilli

METHOD

• In a saucepan, heat the rice bran oil and brown the onion. Place a tajine over gentle heat on the stove. Add the lamb to the onion in the saucepan and season well with salt and pepper. As it cooks, break it up with a wooden spoon.

• When the lamb is evenly browned, add 3 tomatoes, roughly chopped, and 100g pine nuts. Cook for about 5 minutes and for the last of those 5 minutes, add a chopped and seeded red capsicum.

• Now, place a portion of the cooked meat mixture into the tajine base, crack two eggs on top of the meat and top them, in turn, with a sprinkle of Maras chilli.

• Place the tajine, lid in place, in a moderate oven (180 C) for 10 minutes, and that's it. Carefully move from the oven and eat with warmed pita bread.

FATTEH... *a simple seduction*

Fatteh is a deceptively simple dish. But once you have experienced the appeal of this uncomplicated but cleverly layered creation, you will return to it. Again and again. And almost certainly, again.

INGREDIENTS

1kg soaked and cooked chickpeas

1 small tub (150g) tahini dip (Page 12)

¼ tsp crushed garlic

1kg plain yoghurt

1 packet zaatar crisps 🌴

(Oasis, or toast your own by brushing
two pieces of pita bread with olive oil,
sprinkling with zaatar and baking until
crisp and golden – around 5 mins)

1 tsp sea salt

½ tsp mixed spice

½ tsp sumac

garnish

100g pine nuts

100g split, blanched almonds

2 tbs rice bran oil

pinch washed, chopped parsley

METHOD

• Layer the bottom of a deep baking dish with the pita bread crisps.

• Mix the chickpeas with the spices, then spread over the crisps.

• Mix the tahini dip with the yoghurt and the garlic and pour over the chickpeas.

garnish

• Heat the oil in a pan, add the almonds until they colour slightly, add the pine nuts and stir until all the nuts are golden brown. Sprinkle these over the dish.

• Finish by adding the parsley and serve immediately. Do not let the crisps soften.

QUINOA SOUP… *another ancient miracle*

The discovery of quinoa, the ancient grain of the Incas, was, for me, a revelation. I was astonished by its ability to satisfy any appetite for longer than almost anything else. So I experimented with it, and tried interesting new ways to eat it. And when I developed this soup, I found I was eating it almost every day. As, indeed, were my customers at Oasis who now dispatch more than 100 litres of it every week.

INGREDIENTS

1 cup tri-coloured quinoa
(a mixture of red, white and black)

1 cup persian lentils

1 cup green Australian lentils
such as Mount Zero

1 tsp sea salt

1 tsp garlic & herbs 🌴

1 tsp ras el hanout

garnish

red capsicum, chopped
parsley stems, chopped

METHOD

• Rinse the lentils.

• Bring 3 litres water to a boil in a large pot, add the lentils and simmer for 5 minutes.

• Rinse the quinoa well to remove any bitterness. Place in a fine strainer and rinse again. Add to the pot with the lentils.

• Add the spices, return to a boil and simmer gently for about 20 minutes.

• Garnish with chopped red capsicum and parsley stems.

MONK SOUP… *a treat for all seasons*

This soup is traditionally eaten on Good Friday. It is, however, far too good to only eat once a year. However, when I make this soup, my children inevitably pick out the dumplings and eat them. My suggestion, therefore, is to make plenty of them!

INGREDIENTS

500g persian lentils

500g green lentils

1 onion, finely chopped

1 tbs EV olive oil

½ cup plain flour

1 cup fine burghul

½ cup lemon juice

2 tsp sea salt

¼ tsp ground black pepper

¼ tsp ground allspice

1 tsp sumac

½ tsp garlic & herbs 🌿

3 cloves crushed garlic

1 tsp dried mint

METHOD

• To make the dumplings, combine the burghul and the flour with salt, pepper and mint.

• Roll the resulting dough into small (2cm) balls and place them on a lightly oiled oven tray, leaving a gap between each ball.

• Add the persian lentils to a large pot of boiling water and simmer for 10 minutes.

• Add the green lentils, and the spices, return to a boil and continue to simmer for 5 minutes.

• Add the lemon juice, garlic and spices.

• Drop the balls into the boiling mixture, individually, and simmer for 10 minutes.

• In a pan, soften and colour the onion well in hot oil, and add to the soup, stirring.

• When the dumplings are cooked, serve them with the soup.

MAKLOUTA... *a mixed bean blessing*

This hearty soup is earthy and filling. It is unique in terms of the extraordinary array of legumes and grains that go into its meticulous creation. But most important of all, like so many dishes in Lebanese cuisine, it is well worth the effort.

INGREDIENTS

100g chickpeas

100g cannellini beans

100g lima or butter beans

100g borlotti beans

100g kidney beans

100g black-eyed beans

100g laird (large green) lentils

100g red split lentils

100g coarse burghul

100g short-grain rice

1 onion, diced

2 tbs rice bran oil

METHOD

• Wash the chickpeas and beans, cover with water and soak overnight.
The next day, drain and rinse these legumes, add 3 litres of water (or enough to cover the beans) and bring to a boil in a large saucepan. Reduce the heat and simmer the beans for 40 minutes.

• Add the lentils, burghul and rice to the legumes and simmer for a further 15 minutes.

• Add oil in to a hot pan and sauté the onion.
When it has begun to colour, add it to the soup mixture and simmer for a further 2 minutes.

NOTE: Before soaking the legumes overnight, try adding 1 tsp bicarb to soften. Then, rinse them well. This will help them to cook more quickly. If the finished soup is too thick, add water to thin it. In fact, this soup can be adjusted to your preferred consistency.

BARLEY & CHICKPEAS... *killing the chill*

This simple, slow-cooked soup is the perfect winter warmer: it is tasty, satisfying and, for me, redolent of childhood. It is a dish I would help my mother to prepare when I arrived home from school on chilly afternoons. It would cook for hours on end over dying coals and, often, I would burn my tongue, tasting it in my eagerness for it to be ready. But it was worth it.

INGREDIENTS

6 lamb shanks

200g skinless chicken breast fillet cut into 1cm strips

200g pearl barley (rinsed)

100g dried chickpeas, soaked overnight

1 large onion, quartered

1 tsp mixed spice (baharat) 🌴

1 tsp garlic & herbs 🌴

1 tbs sea salt

½ tsp lemon pepper

METHOD

• Place the lamb shanks and onion in a large saucepan and add 3 litres of water. Bring to a gentle boil and skim off any foam that rises to the surface.

• Add the barley, return to a boil and simmer, gently, covered, for 90 minutes.

• Add the chicken, the drained and rinsed chickpeas, the spices and seasoning, return to a boil and simmer for a further 50 minutes, covered, stirring occasionally. Check the seasoning and serve.

SILVERBEET SOUP... *life in a leaf*

This miraculous vegetable – also known as chard or swiss chard – is wholesome, hearty and filling. And in this form, it makes one of the world's most satisfying and nutritious soups – a dish of which I never tire.

INGREDIENTS

500g red lentils

500g green lentils

2 bunches silverbeet, washed and roughly cut into small pieces

1 tbs rice bran oil

1 onion, diced

1 tsp sea salt

1 tsp ground black pepper

1 tsp sumac

juice of a lemon

1 tsp garlic & herbs 🌴

1 tbs rice flour

1 tbs crushed fresh garlic

garnish

fresh parsley or fresh coriander leaves
Maras chilli (optional)

METHOD

• In a large saucepan, colour the onion in the oil.

• Add the silverbeet and the crushed garlic to the onion and continue to cook, stirring, for a further 3 minutes.

• Add the lentils and 6 litres water to the saucepan, bring to a boil and simmer for 10 minutes.

• Add the spices and stir.

• Add the rice flour to thicken the soup slightly. You can add more if you prefer a thicker soup.

• Serve in bowls, and garnish with parsley or coriander leaves, plus Maras chilli if you like a bit more kick.

LENTIL & RICE SOUP... *simple satisfaction*

Now, peep into your larder: nothing to eat? Well, think again, because all you need is rice and lentils, and a few essential spices, and you have the fixings for this delicious soup.

INGREDIENTS

2 cups green lentils, washed

1 cup rice, washed

½ onion, diced

2 tbs rice bran oil

½ tsp salt

½ tsp ras el hanout

½ tsp crushed black pepper

½ tsp mixed spice (baharat) 🌿

garnish

parsley, chopped

METHOD

• Add lentils to large saucepan containing 3 litres boiling water and simmer for 4 minutes.

• Add the rice and spices, then boil for a further 10 minutes.

• Meanwhile, warm the oil in a frying pan and colour the onion.

• Then add the onion to the lentil, rice and spices mix.

• Simmer for another 4 minutes, garnish and serve.

CHICKEN SOUP... *the universal restorative*

In many cultures, including Middle Eastern, a well-made chicken soup is regarded as a wondrous cure for all things. It is often called Jewish penicillin, for example. And unquestionably, when you're not feeling at the top of your game, this soup will provide you with an excellent reason for getting out of bed.

INGREDIENTS

1 whole chicken (jointed and rinsed)

1½ cups rice

3 carrots, peeled and diced

½ onion

sea salt

½ tsp crushed, black pepper

1 tsp ras el hanout

METHOD

• Place chicken pieces in large saucepan with the onion and add 4 litres water.
Bring to a boil and simmer for at least half an hour, skimming as necessary.

• Once it is tender, remove the chicken pieces from the water and remove the meat from the bones.

• Return the chicken meat to the water, add the rice and the spices, the salt and the pepper, return to a boil and simmer for at least 5 minutes.

• Add the carrots, return to a boil and simmer until they too are tender. Then check the seasoning and serve.

TRADITIONAL LEMONADE… *the happiest tipple*

I love this lemonade. I make a vast container of the base cordial at the start of summer, and it never fails to refresh. It is a wonderful beverage to serve for lunch, at any outdoor gathering such as a barbecue, or any time at all, really.

INGREDIENTS

1 cup lemon juice

2 cups caster sugar

½ tsp rose water

METHOD

• In a small bowl, mix the lemon juice, sugar and rose water. Leave it to stand and collect its thoughts on a kitchen bench for a few days, stirring it whenever you walk past.

• When the sugar is dissolved, the mixture is ready. This mixture, incidentally, will keep for up to 2 months in an airtight container.

• To make a glass of lemonade, simply dilute 3 tbs of the lemon mixture with a cup of water and stir. To make a jug of lemonade, follow these same proportions – adding a cup of water for every 3tbs of lemon mixture.

• To serve, wash and slice a lemon and add, with ice, to the jug. Once you have added water to the mixture, you must serve it immediately.

FREEKEH FIG SALAD... *with a tasty splash of colour*

There was a time, whenever I made this dish, that I would carefully peel every fig. I found, however, I was peeling at least 80 figs for a salad requiring just 5 because whenever a family member entered the kitchen, they would begin to eat the figs. So now I simply wash the figs and serve them in their skins. It adds colour to the salad, and maintains the integrity of the figs when you mix it all together. You can substitute chicken for the salmon, incidentally, provided you cook it for longer.

INGREDIENTS

5 fresh figs, rinsed and cut into quarters

2 Lebanese cucumbers, sliced

200g mixed salad leaves

100g dried cranberries

100g flaked almonds

200g freekeh (an ancient grain), rinsed

2 tsp rice bran oil

200g Tasmanian salmon fillet, skin on

2 tsp yallateef 🌴 (Page 5)

2 tbs EV olive oil

2 tbs hibiscus finishing vinegar

2 tbs pomegranate molasses

1 tsp sea salt, pink if available

2 tbs lemon juice

METHOD

• Bring the freekeh to a boil in at least 500ml of water in a large pot, and simmer for 15 minutes. Set aside until the water has been absorbed

• Heat the oil in a hot pan and add the salmon, skin side down, and carefully spread the yallateef on top of the fillet.

• When the fish begins to colour (about 4 minutes, depending upon thickness), carefully turn and cook for 2 more minutes. Take the pan off the heat with the salmon still in place and set aside.

• In a large bowl combine the salad leaves, figs and cucumber slices.

• Prepare the dressing by combining the olive oil, hibiscus finishing vinegar, pomegranate molasses, sea salt and lemon juice. Add the freekeh to the salad, pour the dressing over it and toss well.

• Tip onto a serving dish, break the cooling salmon into bite-sized pieces and place on top of the salad. Garnish with dried cranberries and flaked almonds.

NOTE: This dish can be served warm or cold.

CHICKPEA SALAD... *my simplest pleasure*

We cook more than 100kg of chickpeas every week at Oasis, and use most of them to make hummous. I always put some to one side, however, and use them to throw together this quick and simple salad for lunch – knowing I will enjoy it just as much as I did on the last occasion I ate it, which may have been yesterday.

INGREDIENTS

200g dried chickpeas

1 tsp crushed garlic

½ tsp sea salt

1 large handful finely chopped flat-leaf parsley

1 tomato, diced

lemon juice

½ tsp mixed spice (baharat) 🕷

½ tsp sumac

1 tsp EV olive oil

METHOD

• Soak the chickpeas overnight. Rinse them and cover with cold water, bring to a boil and simmer until just tender (about an hour). Rinse in cold water, strain and put to one side.

• Combine the oil, ½ cup water, salt, garlic, spices and most of the parsley.

• Add this mixture to the chickpeas and mix well.

• Garnish with tomato and the remaining parsley.

TABOULI... *a salad for all seasons*

This classical salad draws its name from taabil – the Arabic word for seasoning. And it is that seasoning that makes it a dish you can eat every day, and never tire of it.

Also, it can be made gluten-free simply by replacing the burghul with quinoa. But remember to rinse the quinoa thoroughly, and to cook it in water until it is tender (about 10 minutes) before draining and adding.

INGREDIENTS

2 bunches flat-leaf parsley, rinsed and dried thoroughly

500g firm tomatoes

1 tbs fine burghul

2 spring onions

a lemon's juice

2 tablespoons EV olive oil

½ teaspoon sea salt

pinch black pepper

pinch mixed spice (baharat) 🌴

pinch tabouli spice 🌴

pinch dried mint

METHOD

• Rinse and dice the tomatoes (5cm cubes). Add the burghul, allowing it time to soak up any liquid.

• Rinse and then chop the spring onions, green and white parts, and add to the tomatoes and burghul. Season with salt and pepper and work in the spices.

• Finely chop the parsley (leaves and thin stems only) and add to the other salad ingredients.

• Add the lemon juice and olive oil and combine well.

PEAR SALAD... *a nutty twist*

Pears are used in salads in many food cultures. But this pear salad is, perhaps, the most surprising of them all. The crispness of the pears and the crunch of the almonds combine brilliantly with the creaminess of the simple, but action-packed, dressing.

INGREDIENTS

1kg pears (firm and hard)

200g mayonnaise

200g cream cheese

½ tsp sea salt

½ tsp dukkah

squeeze lemon or orange juice

100g almond halves

1tbs rice bran oil

garnish

fresh mint leaves

METHOD

• Rinse, core and slice the pears and place in a bowl. Squeeze lemon or orange juice over them to prevent browning. Leave them in the juice for 2 minutes, and then drain.

• Mix the mayonnaise and cream cheese well, and then add, with the dukkah and salt, to the pears and toss together.

• Warm the oil in a hot pan and toast the almonds for 2 minutes.

• Top the salad with the toasted almonds and garnish with the mint leaves.

EGGPLANT SALAD... *smoke and mirrors*

My friend Tamara never really liked eggplant. Until, that is, she tasted this enchanting salad. The smokiness of the roasted eggplant bonds with the tang of the dressing in a perfect marriage of flavours.

INGREDIENTS

2 tbs chopped, flat-leaf parsley

½ red onion, finely sliced

150g cherry tomatoes, halved

2 firm, medium to large eggplants

1 tbs lemon juice

1 tsp sea salt

1 tsp lemon-infused olive oil

½ tsp pomegranate molasses

½ tsp Aleppo pepper

100g pomegranate seeds

METHOD

• Roast the eggplants by placing them directly over a gas flame.

• Turn them carefully with tongs as they blacken and soften. Alternatively, they can be oven-roasted or even seared in a small pan, but the gas flame delivers the best flavour.

• Carefully peel away the blackened skin and cut the eggplant into 3cm cubes.

• Make a dressing by combining the lemon juice, sea salt, lemon-infused olive oil, pomegranate molasses and Aleppo pepper.

• In a bowl, toss the eggplant with the dressing, red onion, tomato and parsley, and garnish with pomegranate seeds and parsley.

POTATO SALAD... *playing with flavour*

Is there anybody, anywhere, who does not like potato salad? Probably not. But most home cooks have their own approach to the dish, and this is mine. I keep my recipes simple, but I continually strive for flavour twists. Here, I rely on oil flavours to bring the changes.

INGREDIENTS

1kg potatoes, washed and peeled

½ bunch spring onions, washed and roughly chopped

½ red onion, finely chopped

1 tbs EV olive oil

1 tbs walnut oil

3 fresh mint leaves, finely cut

½ tsp Maras chilli

½ tsp sea salt

½ tsp black pepper

4 stalks parsley, chopped, leaves only

½ tsp sweet paprika

¼ red capsicum, seeds and pith removed, roughly chopped

METHOD

• Bring a pot of water to a boil.

• Dice the potatoes into 2cm cubes, bring them to a boil in lightly salted water and boil for 3 minutes.

• Remove from the heat, but leave the potatoes in the water for 5 minutes before draining.

• Place the oils, onion, herbs and spices (excluding sweet paprika) in a large bowl and mix well.

• Add the potatoes to this mixture and toss well.

• Serve, garnished with capsicum, parsley and sweet paprika.

FARRO SALAD... *a wise old wheat*

Farro is another of those ancient grains, essentially a wheat variety, that has re-entered our lives, and has some rather unique properties in terms of digestibility. My daughter introduced me to it by making this salad for me, and now I'm hooked. This is easily my favourite way to eat farro. Serve it on its own, warm or cold, or as a side dish with meat if you prefer.

INGREDIENTS

400g farro (a whole grain)

1 tbs rice bran oil

300g Archie's blend 2 🌴

dressing

1 tbs EV olive oil

1 tbs hibiscus dressing

1tbs apple balsamic vinegar

1 tsp soy sauce

1 tsp garlic dip 🌴

1 tsp Maras chilli

1 tsp garlic & herbs 🌴

1 tbs lemon juice

1 tsp mustard with seeds

1 tsp sea salt

1 tsp crushed pepper

1 tsp zaatar

METHOD

• Bring farro to a boil in a saucepan with twice its own volume of water and simmer for 10 minutes.

• Drain off any remaining liquid and set grain aside.

• Heat oil in a pan, heat Archie's blend for 2 minutes and set aside.

• Make a dressing by mixing the ingredients and, in a large bowl, combine the farro, Archie's blend and the dressing. Mix well and serve.

POMEGRANATE–WALNUT SALAD... *all that glisters*

Jewel-like pomegranate seeds appear in many of my dishes. But in this wonderfully simple salad, pomegranate becomes the hero. The tang of the seeds balances the salad's warm and seductive dressing, and the colours are hypnotic – which is why this photogenic dish was picked to star on the cover.

INGREDIENTS

200g mixed salad leaves, washed

100g walnuts, whole

200g tomatoes, roughly chopped

small bunch radishes, sliced

1 tbs pomegranate molasses

1 tbs balsamic fig vinegar

1 tbs hibiscus finishing vinegar

1 tbs EV olive oil

1 tbs crushed garlic

1 tsp sea salt

1 tsp sumac

150g pomegranate seeds

METHOD

• Mix oil, garlic, pomegranate molasses, balsamic fig vinegar, hibiscus finishing vinegar, salt and sumac in a small bowl to create a dressing.

• Place the salad leaves, tomato and walnuts in a large bowl.

• Pour the dressing over the salad and toss thoroughly.

• Serve with the pomegranate seeds sprinkled on top.

NOTE: Pomegranates are seasonal.
If they are unavailable, dried barberries are a good substitute.

MAFTOUL SALAD... *it's all in the tang*

Maftoul is yet another member of the couscous family. But unlike instant couscous, maftoul needs to be boiled briefly, and has a texture not unlike al dente pasta. It is smaller than moghrabieh, however, but larger than Israeli couscous. And presented in this way, it makes a delectable salad with a warm, tangy dressing to balance the crispness of the nuts and vegies.

INGREDIENTS

1 x 400g bag maftoul

1 tbs avocado oil

2 tbs hibiscus finishing vinegar

2 tbs lemon juice

1 tbs fig balsamic vinegar

½ tbs pomegranate molasses

1 tbs crushed garlic

1 tbs dried mint

½ bag Archie's blend 2 🌱

1 red onion, finely sliced

½ bunch radishes, washed and sliced

salad leaves as required, washed and dried

sea salt and pepper

handful fresh basil leaves

METHOD

• Bring the maftoul to a boil in plenty of salted water and simmer for 5 minutes; drain and set aside.

• In a large bowl, mix the avocado oil, hibiscus finishing vinegar, lemon juice, fig balsamic, pomegranate molasses, basil leaves, garlic and mint.

• Add Archie's blend 2, radishes and onion.

• Add the maftoul and toss together.

• Fold through the salad leaves and the basil.
Toss well to dress.

• Serve with a sprinkle of Archie's blend 2.

FATTOUSH... *the crunch of summer*

This popular salad is traditionally served in summer when all of the ingredients are at their best. The zaatar crisps are especially good just as they begin to soak up the dressing.

INGREDIENTS

1kg tomato (chopped)

1kg cucumber (sliced)

½ bunch spring onions (chopped)

½ bunch purslane leaves

½ bunch flat-leaf parsley
(chopped, leaves only)

½ bunch fresh mint
(chopped, leaves only)

1 bunch radishes, halved

2 tbs sumac

1 tbs pomegranate molasses

1 tbs sea salt

2-3 lemons (juiced)

2 tbs EV olive oil

1-2 packets zaatar crisps 🌴 *

*Or toast your own by brushing
two pieces of pita bread with olive oil,
sprinkling with zaatar and baking until
crisp and golden – around 5 mins

METHOD

• Place the vegetables in a bowl with the spices, lemon juice and oil and toss together thoroughly.

• So they remain crunchy, add the crisps just before serving.

GRILLED VEGETABLE SALAD... *char, char, char*

Char-grilling vegetables endows them with a smoky tang that can be achieved in no other way. Try serving this dish alongside grilled meats or fish at your next barbecue: it's wholesome, tasty and surprisingly substantial.

INGREDIENTS

2 tomatoes, quartered

200g okra, whole

200g cauliflower, broken into florets

100g snow peas, topped and tailed, strings removed

1 tsp crushed garlic

1 tsp rice bran oil

1 tsp oyster sauce

1 tsp soy

½ tsp sea salt

dressing

½ tsp pomegranate molasses

½ tsp lemon-infused EV olive oil

½ tsp Maras chilli

½ tsp seeded mustard

½ tsp zaatar

1 tbs lemon juice

METHOD

• Wash the vegetables. In a large bowl, combine the tomatoes, cauliflower and okra with the garlic, ½ tsp rice bran oil and salt. Toss well.

• Char-grill or barbecue the tomato, okra and cauliflower until black grill marks are evident and they are starting to soften. Set aside to cool.

• Add ½ tsp rice bran oil to a hot pan. Add the snow peas and cook briskly, tossing, for 2 minutes. Add oyster sauce and soy. Toss for 2 minutes. Remove from heat.

• Tip into a large bowl, along with any liquid from the pan, and set aside to cool.

• In a small bowl, mix the dressing ingredients. Pour this dressing over the vegetables and gently fold through. Serve warm or cold.

PUMPKIN & CHICORY SALAD... *a happy combo*

Like so many things I love to cook, I stumbled upon this combination while preparing other dishes. Chicory, as a fresh leaf, can be bitter. It becomes sweeter, however, when it is blanched. While it works beautifully in this combination, it is also worth noting the pumpkin and pine nut mixture makes a delicious hot dish in its own right.

INGREDIENTS

½ tsp Maras chilli

½ tsp black pepper

½ tsp sea salt

½ tsp mixed spice (baharat)

1 large onion, sliced

4 cloves garlic, finely sliced

½ bunch fresh basil,
coarsely chopped or torn

1 tbs EV olive oil

50g pine nuts

1 pumpkin (2kg)

1 bunch chicory, coarsely chopped

dressing

½ tsp sea salt

½ tsp lemon-infused olive oil

½ tsp grape balsamic vinegar

½ tsp sesame oil

METHOD

• Set an oven to 180 C. Wash and seed the pumpkin and cut into 3cm chunks, leaving the skin on. Place in a baking dish.

• Add the spices, basil, onion, garlic, pine nuts and oil to the pumpkin. Mix well and place in the oven for 30 minutes. Set aside to cool.

• Wash the chicory at least 3 times and, in a large saucepan, bring a litre of water to a boil and simmer the chicory for 20 minutes. Drain it thoroughly.

• In a large bowl, mix the dressing components well, add the pumpkin mixture and then fold through the chicory. Serve cold.

COUSCOUS SALAD… *Moroccan versatility*

This refreshing dish, from Morocco, is ideal for the sort of weather you are likely to encounter in that magical kingdom. It is quick and easy to make, filling enough to serve as a meal, or light enough for a side dish.

INGREDIENTS

200g instant couscous

2tbs + 1 dash EV olive oil

1 Lebanese cucumber, diced

½ onion, finely sliced

1 capsicum, seeds and pith removed, diced

2 tomatoes, diced

½ head lettuce, roughly chopped

¼ bunch flat-leaf parsley, chopped (leaves only)

2 tbs lemon juice

½ tsp crushed garlic

½ tsp garlic dip 🌴

1 tsp pomegranate molasses

1 tbs hibiscus dressing

1 tbs apple balsamic vinegar

sea salt and freshly-ground black pepper

1 x 400g can chickpeas, drained and rinsed

pinch dried rose petals

METHOD

• Place couscous in a large bowl. Bring 200ml water plus a dash of olive oil to a boil and pour over couscous.

• Set aside, uncovered, for 5-10 minutes.

• In a large bowl combine the remaining olive oil, lemon juice, pomegranate molasses, hibiscus dressing, apple balsamic vinegar, crushed garlic and garlic dip, and mix well.
Add the chickpeas and vegetables.

• Fluff couscous with a fork and season with salt and pepper. Add to the salad and dressing mix and stir well to combine.

• Sprinkle with parsley and garnish with dried rose petals. Serve with a tajine, or eat it on its own.

POMEGRANATE SUNRISE... *good health in a glass*

Pomegranate seeds are exquisitely pretty, even jewel-like. But they are also life-enhancing: high in anti-oxidants, and have shown promise as an ally in the fight against cancer. A 30ml shot of pomegranate juice taken daily, also, may assist in lowering blood pressure. And if you take it in the form of this drink, early on a summer's day, it will also put a smile on your face.

INGREDIENTS

2 fresh pomegranates, seeds only

4 tsp pomegranate syrup

2 tsp pomegranate molasses

small handful fresh mint leaves

500g sparkling mineral water

ice

METHOD

• Muddle together half the pomegranate seeds and half the mint.

• Pass through a fine sieve into a serving jug and discard the solids.

• Add the pomegranate molasses and syrup and mix well.

• Add the sparkling mineral water and stir.

• Add the remaining pomegranate seeds and fresh mint.

• Add ice, stir again, and serve.

TRADITIONAL RICE… *feeding a family*

As a young and conscientious mother, I liked to load up the family table with a range of nutritious and delicious food. But much of the time, all my young children would eat was traditional rice, with or without yoghurt. When you taste this dish – which works as a supporting act or the star attraction – you will probably understand why.

INGREDIENTS

2 cups basmati rice, ideally the par-boiled one from Oasis

200g egg noodles

2 tbs rice bran oil

1 tbs sea salt

1 tsp hawaij (a Yemeni spice mixture)

METHOD

• Heat the oil in a saucepan and fry the egg noodles until golden.

• Rinse the rice then add to the egg noodles; stir well to combine.

• Add 4 cups water and stir while adding the sea salt and hawaij.

• Cover, and allow to simmer on a low heat until all the water has been absorbed.

• Once the rice is tender, remove from the heat and rest for five minutes before serving.

CAULI & CARROT IN TAHINI… *a happy marriage*

There was cauliflower in the larder, and there were crisp carrots. My plan was to combine them in a creamy dish using tahini paste – a Middle Eastern cauliflower cheese, if you like. The result, however, was even more successful than I had anticipated: a regular customer tasted it and ordered six servings immediately. She still buys it regularly. It is, she insists, the only way she can persuade her lactose-intolerant children to eat vegetables.

INGREDIENTS

1 onion, diced

3 tbs rice bran oil
(more if frying the cauliflower)

¼ cup fresh coriander leaves, chopped

3 large carrots, sliced

2 tbs tahini paste

½ tsp sea salt

½ tsp ras el hanout

½ tsp garlic & herbs 🌴

½ tsp lemon pepper

2 tbs rice flour

1 cauliflower, divided into florets

parsley to garnish

METHOD

• In a large saucepan, heat 1 tbs rice bran oil and colour the onion. Add the coriander and the sliced carrot. Stir.

• Add the spices and cook for 5 minutes.

• Add 1 litre water and stir, add the tahini paste, add the rice flour to thicken and mix well to eliminate lumps. Add this to the carrots.

• Toss the cauliflower with 2 tbs oil and bake for 20 minutes at 180 C. Or, if you prefer, deep fry in oil.

• Tip the carrots and sauce into a serving dish and top with the cauliflower.

• Garnish with parsley and serve the dish with traditional rice, or on its own.

MOUJADARA... *for the enlightened peasant*

This dish is, in every sense, peasant food – a tasty and nutritious belly-filler for manual workers. It has, over the centuries, proven its worth as a food that will fuel labourers throughout their working day while holding their interest, and is traditionally cooked in a large terracotta pot. But it also happens to be absolutely delicious.

INGREDIENTS

2 cups lentils
(Australian green lentils,
such as those from Mt Zero
in Victoria, work well,
and their freshness adds
to the dish)

2 cups coarse burghul (rinsed)

1 small onion (diced)

1 small onion (slivered)

4 tbs rice bran oil

½ tsp sea salt

½ tsp mixed spice (baharat) 🌴

½ tsp Maras chilli

garnish

pickled turnips 🌴

METHOD

• Simmer the lentils in at least six cups of unsalted water until tender – around 15 minutes.

• Drain the lentils over a bowl and reserve 4 cups of the cooking liquid.

• In a large pot, add the lentils and burghul to the reserved cooking liquid, place over low heat.

• In a pan, fry the slivered onion in oil until brown and crisp.

• Remove the onion to paper kitchen towels to drain. Reserve the oil.

• Fry the diced onions in the oil until they begin to brown.

• Tip the diced onions and oil into the lentil mixture.

• Season with salt and spices to taste.

• Bring to simmer for 2 minutes, cover, and remove from heat – allowing the water to be absorbed.

• Serve with the crisp onions.

• Garnish with the crisp, slivered onion and the pickled turnips. Serve with fattoush (Page 67) or tabouli (Page 52).

BUCKWHEAT & VEGETABLES... *the good seed*

Western diets tend towards the acidic. Buckwheat, however, can help to achieve and maintain a healthy pH balance. This simple recipe is a delicious way to combine buckwheat – a seed rather than a cereal, and a neglected staple – with fresh vegetables. But by all means add meat to the dish and, if you are feeling particularly adventurous, some yallateef, also.

INGREDIENTS

2 cups buckwheat

2 tbs rice bran oil

1 large onion, roughly sliced

2 carrots, roughly sliced

2 zucchini, roughly sliced

250g pitted Kalamata olives

1 tsp ras el hanout

½ tsp Moroccan dukkah 🌴

½ tsp hawaij (Yemeni spice mix)

1 tsp carob molasses

½ tsp charlic (red and green chillies pickled in garlic and oil) 🌴

1 tsp sea salt

METHOD

• Sweat the onion and carrot in oil in a large saucepan for about 8 minutes.

• Add the olives and zucchini and cook for 2 more minutes.

• Add the spices and stir to combine well.

• Add 6 cups water, bring the mixture to a boil and add the buckwheat. Simmer for a minute longer.

• Remove from the heat and set aside for about 15 minutes, or until very little water is left.

VEGETARIAN OKRA… *a new playmate*

Okra is unfamiliar to many Australians: I face endless questions about it when I serve it at Oasis. But in brief, it is a versatile and distinctive vegetable. It is available in a variety of sizes, fresh and frozen. And it is well worth playing with. In addition to this simple approach, for example, I marinate okra in garlic and oil and grill it on a barbecue before serving it on tomatoes, as with this dish, and mopping up the sauce.

INGREDIENTS

1kg fresh okra
(or 1kg frozen okra, which you
need to deep-fry, briefly, and
add after the tomato)

2 onions, slivered

4 cloves garlic, finely sliced

500g fresh tomatoes, cut into quarters

4 tbs rice bran oil

1 cup tomato purée

½ tsp sea salt

½ tsp crushed black pepper

½ tsp mixed spice (baharat) 🌴

½ tsp Maras chilli

METHOD

• Heat oil in a pan, add the onion and the garlic.

• Add the okra and cook for 5 minutes, stirring occasionally.

• Add the fresh tomato and the spices and cook for another 5 minutes.

• Add the tomato purée, bring to a boil and cook for 2 minutes.

• Serve hot or cold.

POMEGRANATE JEWELLED RICE... *as pretty as*

A chance encounter with this entrancing dish can make it difficult to be satisfied with plain rice, ever again. The nuts, berries and dried fruit deliver spectacular flavour bursts, and the jewel-like pomegranate beads make it look like a dish you could wear as well as eat.

INGREDIENTS

100g barberries

100g cashews, unsalted and roasted

100g slivered almonds

100g raw pistachio kernels

100g pumpkin seed kernels

100g sunflower seed kernels

100g dried apricots, thinly sliced

1 tbs yallateef 🌴 (Page 5)

1 tsp zhug

2 tbs pomegranate molasses

3 tbs rice bran oil

2 cups basmati rice, rinsed

1 pinch saffron threads

1 tsp sea salt

100g fresh pomegranate seeds (seasonal; more barberries can be used when these are not available)

METHOD

• Warm the oil in a large saucepan; add the nuts and the dried fruit, and stir until the nuts begin to colour.

• Add the yallateef, pomegranate molasses and zhug. Stir.

• Add the rice and mix well.

• Add 4 cups boiling water, salt and saffron threads, stir.

• Simmer for 5 minutes and then remove from the heat.

• Cover until all the liquid is absorbed (about 20 minutes).

• Transfer to a serving plate or bowl.

• Garnish with fresh pomegranate seeds.

• Serve on its own, with yoghurt or to accompany a meat dish.

LOUBIEH BI ZEIT... *bean there, loved this*

My youngest son developed something close to an obsession with this dish through high school. He would request it before he left for school, and I would have it ready for him when he arrived home. Whereupon he would demolish it – wiping his plate clean with pita bread. But now? Yes, he still loves it...

INGREDIENTS

1 onion, diced

4 garlic cloves, finely chopped

1.5kg flat green beans, chopped or simply snapped

3 tbs rice bran oil

2 x 400g cans tomatoes or 6 fresh Roma tomatoes, coarsley chopped

1 tbs sea salt

½ tsp cracked black pepper

½ tsp mixed spice (baharat)

½ tsp dry mint or chopped fresh mint

1 x 400g can lima beans

METHOD

• Heat the oil in a saucepan and sauté the onions until golden. Add the garlic.

• Add the green beans, cook on a low heat for 10-15 minutes, stirring occasionally. Add the canned beans and spices. Stir to combine.

• Cover and bring to simmer.

• Add the tomatoes and continue to simmer for 5 minutes.

• Serve hot or cold with, my son would insist, plenty of pita bread.

MOGHRABIEH... *a seductive Lebanese couscous*

Moghrabieh – the word means a dish from the Maghreb – consists of small, firm, pasta-like balls. This interpretation of the Lebanese classic, you will find, is addictive, and can lead to intemperate behaviour – including, but not limited to, licking your plate clean.

INGREDIENTS

1 large onion, chopped

1 tbs rice bran oil

1 tsp sea salt

½ tsp moghrabieh spice 🌴

½ tsp garlic & herbs 🌴

½ tsp dried mint

½ tsp Aleppo pepper

1 tsp zhug

1 x 400g can chickpeas, drained and rinsed

300g cherry tomatoes

2 tbs chopped parsley

1kg moghrabieh (Lebanese couscous)

1 large sweet potato, peeled and diced into 2cm cubes

METHOD

• Add the moghrabieh to 3 litres of boiling water and cook for 15 minutes; drain.

• Heat the oil in a large saucepan and add the onion. After 2 minutes add the sweet potato and cook for 10 minutes.

• Add all the spices, chickpeas and parsley.

• Add 1 cup water and bring to a boil.

• Add the moghrabieh, stir to combine well, add the cherry tomatoes and cook for 2 minutes.

• Serve on its own or with chicken with yallateef (Page 125).

QUINOA-STUFFED CAPSICUMS... *vegie triumph*

When my daughter decided, as daughters do, to turn vegetarian, it encouraged me to become more creative with non-meat ingredients. This is a dish I developed and it has become a firm favourite for all family members – even the carnivores. You will find the unusual spice mixes/exotic ingredients at Oasis, naturally.

INGREDIENTS

1 cup quinoa, rinsed thoroughly and simmered, covered, for about 15 minutes.

6 large capsicums

3 tbs rice bran oil

1 onion, grated

1 tbs pulp from grilled garlic cloves

1 tsp sea salt

1 tbs Tunisian dukkah 🌴

¼ tsp Aleppo pepper

¼ tsp "morerocken" seasoning 🌴

¼ tsp cayenne pepper

¼ tsp sweet paprika

¼ tsp ground cumin

¼ tsp herbs de provence

¼ tsp melange classique

¼ tsp garlic & herbs 🌴

¼ tsp hot desert sand 🌴

½ tsp zhug

2 carrots, grated

2 turnips, grated

2 potatoes, grated

200g pumpkin, grated

1 x 500g jar mixed mushrooms

100g pitted Kalamata olives

100g unsalted, roasted cashews

METHOD

• Heat oil in a saucepan; add onion, garlic and mushrooms.

• Add all the spices and stir to combine.

• Gradually add the grated vegetables; mix thoroughly and cook for 5-10 minutes.

• Take off the heat; add quinoa, olives and cashews.

• Wash the capsicums and carefully cut a "lid" into each, leaving it hinged on one side. Remove the seeds and pith.

• Carefully fill the capsicums with the stuffing mixture.

• In a second saucepan, make the sauce by adding the diced tomato, 2 cups boiling water, salt, black pepper, mint and rice flour. Heat and simmer, stirring.

• Place the capsicums with the sauce in a baking dish and cover with foil. Bake at 180 C for 15 minutes.

• Remove the foil and bake for 15 minutes more.

• Baste well with the sauce and serve.

sauce

2 x 400g cans diced tomatoes

1 tsp rice flour

1 tsp sea salt

1 tsp crushed black pepper

1 tsp dried mint

EGGPLANT MADNESS…*warmth from within*

This wholesome and substantial dish will give special meaning to cold days. In fact, this creation may encourage you to put out the welcome mat for winter.

INGREDIENTS

4 eggplants, diced (2cm cubes), salted and set aside for 5 minutes

2 carrots, diced

2 potatoes, diced (2cm cubes)

1 onion, diced

2 cloves garlic, finely sliced

200g dried chickpeas (soak overnight, rinse, bring to a boil, simmer for 20 minutes and drain)

2 tbs rice bran oil

½ tsp sea salt

1 tbs yallateef 🌴 (Page 5)

½ tsp garlic & herbs 🌴

½ tsp crushed pepper

½ tsp Maras chilli

3 x 400g cans crushed tomato

METHOD

• Heat the oil in a saucepan. Colour the onion (about 4 minutes) and then add the garlic and cook for a further minute, stirring constantly.

• Add the potato, carrots and cooked chickpeas and cook for 5 more minutes.

• Add the eggplant and the spices and cook for another 5 minutes.

• Add the tomato. Bring mixture to a boil and simmer for another 2 minutes to thicken.

• Allow to rest briefly before serving.

VEGIE BURGHUL… *three wise ingredients*

Dishes do not come any simpler, any less complicated, than this one. But, curiously, it is a satisfying combination of which you will never tire. Trust me...

INGREDIENTS

½ tbs yallateef 🌴 (Page 5)

2 cups coarse Turkish burghul, rinsed

½ onion, diced

1 bunch spinach, washed and coarsely chopped (or a large handful baby spinach, washed)

2 tbs rice bran oil

1 tsp sea salt

½ tsp hawaij (Yemeni spice mix)

1 x 400g can cooked chickpeas (or 250g dried chickpeas soaked overnight, rinsed and simmered for an hour)

METHOD

• Place the onion in a saucepan and fry in the rice bran oil, stirring until the onions are translucent. Add the yallateef.

• Add the burghul and stir. Add the chickpeas and hawaij and stir to combine. Add 4 cups of room temperature water and salt. Bring to a boil and simmer for 3 minutes.

• Remove from the heat, add the spinach and mix well. Cover and rest for 10 minutes to allow the water to be absorbed.

• Serve as a side dish, or as a splendid meal with tzatziki.

YAKHANEH... *more vegie magic*

This vegetarian dish is great served on top of traditional rice (Page 78). If you prefer to eat it on its own, thicken it with 1 tsp of rice flour which can be added with the peas. Be sure to stir it in thoroughly, however, to prevent lumps from forming.

INGREDIENTS

½kg potatoes, washed, diced (2cm cubes)

2 carrots, diced

250g frozen peas

1 onion, diced

1 tsp sea salt

½ tsp dried mint

1 tbs rice bran oil

2 tbs tomato paste

6 tomatoes, quartered

¼ tsp garam masala

¼ tsp sweet paprika

¼ tsp crushed black pepper

1 tsp sea salt

¼ tsp Aleppo pepper

METHOD

• In a medium saucepan, heat the oil and add the onion; sweat until translucent. Add the potato and carrots and cook for 5 minutes, stirring constantly.

• Add the fresh tomato and spices. Stir well and add 2.5 litres water.

• Bring to a boil and simmer for 3 minutes.

• Add the tomato paste and the peas; return to a boil and simmer for a further 3 minutes.

• Serve when the potato is cooked through.

EGGPLANT WITH YALLATEEF... *a touch of class*

Eggplant was never a favourite of mine: as a child, I found it lacking in flavour. But when, finally, I added yallateef – the miraculous condiment that has provided this book with a title – I began, suddenly, to crave eggplant. And I still do. Try this dish with quinoa rice, (Page 102) or simply eat it on its own. Often...

INGREDIENTS

2 eggplants, cut into 2cm thick discs

2 onions, cut into wedges

2 garlic cloves, finely sliced

3 fresh tomatoes, coarsely chopped

300g yallateef 🌴 (Page 5)

1 tsp rice bran oil

sea salt (plenty)

¼ tsp Aleppo pepper

¼ tsp garlic & herbs 🌴

¼ tsp tajine spice 🌴

¼ tsp kabsa spice 🌴

METHOD

• Rub salt into both sides of the cut eggplant discs; this prevents them becoming discoloured. Leave to stand for 10 minutes.

• Heat 1 tsp of rice bran oil in a pan and cook the onion and the garlic, together, for 2 minutes. Add the tomatoes and the spices and simmer for 5 minutes to create a sauce.

• Oil the eggplant, place in an ovenproof dish and cook in the oven for 10 minutes at 180 C.

• Spread 1 tbs of yallateef over the eggplant slices.

• Spread the tomato sauce over a baking tray and position the eggplant slices on top. Bake for 15 minutes.

QUINOA RICE… *the best of two worlds*

Rice is a miraculous staple. But combine it with ancient quinoa and the combination rises to new heights. This dish, eaten on its own, is memorable. But served with a suitable meat course, it is unforgettable.

INGREDIENTS

2 cups par-boiled basmati rice (Oasis, or wash, blanch and drain the basmati rice before using)

2 cups quinoa

1 x 400g can black beans

2 tbs rice bran oil

½ onion

1 tsp sea salt

½ tsp ras el hanout

¼ bunch parsley, chopped

METHOD

• Heat oil in a saucepan and saute the onion until golden.

• Add the parsley, ras el hanout, beans and salt.

• Rinse the rice and quinoa well and add to the saucepan. Stir until well combined.

• Add 5 cups water, continuing to stir.

• Cover, and allow to simmer until all of the water has been absorbed.

• When the rice is tender, remove from the heat and allow to rest, covered, for five minutes before serving.

VEGIE PARCELS... *a possible dream*

I am not food-obsessed, honestly. But I actually dreamed, one night, about making these tasty parcels, which I had never made before. So I went to work, threw together a dough, and had them finished by lunchtime. Whereupon they all disappeared. Magic.

INGREDIENTS

pastry

2kg plain flour

½ cup rice bran oil

1 tsp sugar

¼ tsp sea salt

1 tsp dried yeast

vegies

½ tsp rice bran oil

½ onion, finely chopped

500g pumpkin, cut into 1cm cubes

2 red capsicum, seeds and pith removed and cut into 1cm cubes

2 carrots, cut into 1cm cubes

2 potatoes, washed, cut into 1cm cubes

½ bunch parsley, washed and chopped (leaves only)

50g pine nuts

½ tsp sea salt

½ tsp garlic & herbs 🌴

½ tsp Maras chilli

¼ tsp ras el hanout

sesame seeds

METHOD

pastry

• Mix ingredients with 1 litre warm water and knead for about 15 minutes.

• Then, wrap in plastic wrap and set aside for 1 hour to rest at room temperature. Any leftover pastry can be refrigerated or even frozen.

vegies

• Heat oven to 180 C.

• Heat oil in a large pan, add the onion and cook for 2 minutes.

• Add the potato and cook for 2 more minutes, stirring.

• Add the carrots and cook for 2 more minutes, stirring.

• Add the pumpkin and cook for 2 more minutes.

• Add the parsley, capsicum, pine nuts and spices; cook for 2 more minutes, stirring constantly. Take off the heat and set aside to cool.

• Roll out the dough to a thickness of 2.5mm and cut into 20cm diameter discs.

• Place ½ cup of the vegetable mixture at the centre of each disc, bring the opposite sides together, joining them where they meet. If necessary, apply a little water to help the dough stick.

• Carefully position the parcels on a baking tray. Brush the tops with rice bran oil and sprinkle with sesame seeds.

• Bake them for 30 minutes, or until they are golden. Allow to cool before serving.

SPICY WHOLE FISH... *flavour, texture and bones*

Yallateef is an ingredient I developed, originally, as a stuffing for this dish. The nuts and the spices worked so well together, however, that it became a combination I would use in many other recipes. Eventually, it found its way onto the Oasis shelves as a dish in its own right. Cooking fish whole, as we do here, provides additional flavour and texture, but be careful: whole fish, not unreasonably, have bones. You can apply this method to any whole fish that you enjoy.

INGREDIENTS

fish

1 trevally, snapper or similar whole fish (1-1½kg)

¼ tsp sea salt

350g yallateef 🌴 (Page 5)

½ cup lemon juice

garnish

2 tbs rice bran oil

200g pine nuts

chopped flat-leaf parsley, leaves only

2 lemons, washed and sliced

METHOD

• Set an oven to 180 C.

• Wash the fish thoroughly, inside and out. Pat dry.

• Score the skin of the fish with a sharp knife and rub in sea salt.

• Stuff the fish with yallateef.

• Place in an ovenproof dish, cover with foil and bake for 35 minutes.

• Lift the dish from the oven, uncover the fish, add the lemon juice and return to the oven, uncovered, for 5 minutes.

• While the fish is cooking, prepare pine nuts for the garnish by heating the oil in a frying pan and sautéing them until golden brown (about 5 minutes).

• Garnish with the pine nuts, parsley and lemon slices, and serve with tahini dip on the side.

SPICY RICE... *meat or sweet*

Traditional or Lebanese rice is a family favourite. But this lively variation introduces different textures and flavours with meat and nuts. You can make it without the meat, of course, and add more nuts instead. Or you can add dried fruit or berries to make it sweeter.

INGREDIENTS

250g lamb topside, diced (1cm cubes)

2 cups basmati rice, washed well

2 onions, diced

½ tsp mixed spice (baharat) 🌴

½ tsp ras el hanout

100g pine nuts

100g split almonds

2 tbs rice bran oil

½ tsp sea salt

¼ tsp Maras chilli

METHOD

• Heat oil in a deep pan with a lid, or in a saucepan, and sweat the onions until translucent (2 minutes).

• Increase the heat, add the lamb, sea salt, mixed spice, Maras chilli and ras el hanout, stirring, and sauté until the meat is cooked.

• Add the almonds for two minutes. Toss, and then add the pine nuts and toss until they darken slightly.

• Add the rice to this mixture, stir, and add 4 cups boiling water. Cook for 3 minutes.

• Cover the pan and set aside for 20 minutes, or until all the water is absorbed.

LAMB COUSCOUS... *light yet rich*

Instant couscous, as a side dish, is often prepared simply by adding boiling water or stock, allowing it to absorb the liquid, and fluffing it with a fork. The method I use here, however, allows it to absorb an array of flavours. This dish has all the lightness of couscous, but with the richness of lamb stew. In fact, it can be made with any meat you choose.

INGREDIENTS

2 cups instant couscous

2 tsp rice bran oil

500g lamb (backstrap), diced (2.5cm cubes)

1 onion, roughly chopped

2 cloves garlic, finely sliced

1 tbs fresh coriander leaves, chopped

¼ tsp turmeric

¼ tsp hawaij

¼ tsp ras el hanout

1 tsp sea salt

2 x 400g cans whole tomatoes

200g pitted olives

1 x 400g can red beans

1 capsicum, freshly roasted, peeled and seeded (or from a jar of roasted capsicums, sliced into strips)

50g dried rose petals

100g flaked almonds

METHOD

• Heat oil in a large saucepan and add the onion, garlic and coriander. Sweat, stirring, for 2 minutes.

• Add lamb and spices, increase heat and sauté for 5 minutes.

• Add tomato, olives, beans and 4 cups hot water. Bring to a boil.

• Turn off heat and add couscous. Stir well to combine.

• Set aside, covered, for 15 minutes to allow couscous to absorb sauce.

• Take one roasted capsicum and slice into strips.

• Spoon the lamb couscous into a serving dish. Garnish with rose petals, almonds and the slices of roasted capsicum.

NOTE: You can roast your own capsicum over a gas flame, turning it carefully with tongs as it blackens and softens. Place in a bowl, cover with cling wrap and set aside for 15 minutes. Unwrap and peel: the skin will come off easily, but run it under cold water as you peel it, if that helps. Discard seeds and pulp before slicing.

KAFTA IN TAHINI... *changing the pace*

This is a stunning alternative to the more familiar presentation of kafta in a tomato sauce. In this version, a tahini sauce keeps the kafta seductively moist. This dish, served with fattoush (Page 67), makes an impeccably balanced meal.

INGREDIENTS

kafta

1kg lean lamb, minced

1 large onion, trimmed and peeled

1 bunch flat-leaf parsley

1 tsp sea salt

½ tsp freshly ground black pepper

½ tsp kafta spice 🌴

sauce

3 tbs tahini paste

½ tsp salt

1 tbs lemon juice

½ tsp white pepper

garnish

½ onion, thinly sliced

1 tsp rice bran oil

1 tsp flat-leaf parsley, leaves only, finely chopped

METHOD

• To make the kafta, set your oven at 180 C. Rinse and dry the parsley, removing the stems and discarding. Reserve enough leaves for the garnish.

• Quarter the onion and place in a food processor. Process for a few seconds. Add the unreserved parsley leaves and process to a fine, even blend. Add the spices and pulse a couple of times. Place this mixture in a bowl, add the mince and combine well with your hands.

• Wet your hands in cold water to prevent the meat sticking. Shape the kafta into 3cm balls, and then flatten each ball into a disc, 1cm thick. Position these discs in an oiled, ovenproof dish and place in the oven.

• Whisk the sauce ingredients together with 1 cup water in a bowl to achieve a smooth mixture, free of lumps.

• Lift the kafta from the oven after 20 minutes, reduce the oven temperature to 140 C, cover with the sauce and return to the oven for 10 minutes.

• For the garnish, heat the oil in a pan and sauté the onions for 10 minutes, or until they are golden. Drain them on paper kitchen towels.

• Top the kafta with the onions and finish with the parsley.

GARLIC CHICKEN & POTATOES... *please the crowds*

This quick and simple dish is one of the most popular served in our cafe. It also seems to be hugely popular with home cooks who can assemble it quickly, effortlessly, and at the last minute.

INGREDIENTS

1kg potatoes

6-8 chicken drumsticks

1 clove garlic, peeled

1 tbs rice bran oil

juice 3 lemons

1 tsp shish tawook 🌴

1 tsp sumac

½ tsp zaatar

1 tsp sea salt

METHOD

• Heat oven to 200 C.

• Thoroughly wash potatoes and cut into chunks. Place in a large baking tray with 2 cups water.

• Place drumsticks in a bowl and add shish tawook spice, sea salt and sumac with half the rice bran oil. Mix thoroughly.

• Place the marinated drumsticks on top of the potatoes and bake for 30 minutes.

• Crush the garlic to a paste with the sea salt and mix with the zaatar, lemon juice and the remaining rice bran oil.

• Pour this mixture over the chicken and return the baking tray to the oven for 3 more minutes.

• Remove the finished dish from the oven and serve with rice.

MANSAF… *the world on a platter*

The name of this dish, often considered to be the national dish of Jordan, comes from the Arabic word for large tray or dish. It is often eaten Bedouin-style – with diners standing around a platter of mansaf, scooping it up with their right hands. Traditionally, it is made with fatty meats and lots of butter, but my version is lighter. I serve it with chickpea salad (Page 51) and yoghurt.

INGREDIENTS

5 lamb shanks

1 onion, peeled and quartered

1kg skinless chicken breasts

1 cup yoghurt diluted with ½ cup water

2 cups par-boiled Basmati rice 🕷

1 cup coarse Turkish burghul

1 tsp sea salt

1 tbs mansaf spice 🕷

garnish

100g split, blanched almonds

100g pistachio kernels

50g pine nuts

50g washed, chopped flat-leaf parsley (leaves only)

1 tbs rice bran oil

METHOD

• In a large saucepan, bring 5 litres of water to a boil. Add the lamb shanks and the onion and simmer for 90 minutes, skimming the surface.

• Add the chicken to the saucepan and continue to cook for 30 minutes, skimming carefully.

• Lift out the lamb and chicken, leaving 4½ cups of stock in the saucepan.

• In a small saucepan, bring the diluted yoghurt mixture to a boil, stirring continuously to prevent it from separating. Add this to the meat stock.

• Now add the burghul and rice to the stock; tear the chicken and lamb into small pieces and add it, also.

• Season this mixture with the salt and mansaf spice; cover and simmer for 5 minutes.

• Turn off the heat and set the covered saucepan to one side until all the water has been absorbed. This will take at least 30 minutes.

garnish

• Heat the oil in a frying pan. Add the almonds and, when they begin to colour, add pistachios and pine nuts. Sauté until all are golden brown.

• Garnish with the toasted nuts and a sprinkle of parsley.

STUFFED VINE LEAVES... *hidden treasures*

Making these traditional treasures can be time consuming. And because of this, we make them only for special occasions, and we always make enough to have plenty left over for lunch the following day. But take care: they stay hot in their little overcoats, so serve them with a yoghurt dip or tzatziki (Page 17) in which to cool them down.

INGREDIENTS

400g vine leaves in brine

4 lamb cutlets

500g lamb topside
(finely diced, 5mm cubes)

1½ cups short-grain white rice

2 medium tomatoes, sliced

½ onion (diced)

2 tbs rice bran oil

lemon juice

½ tsp mixed spice (baharat) 🌴

½ tsp dried mint

½ tsp Maras chilli

NOTE: If you prefer to use fresh vine leaves, blanch them in water before using, and add salt, to taste (try a generous pinch each time), to both the stuffing and the water when you add it to the saucepan.

METHOD

• Rinse the vine leaves thoroughly to remove excess salt.

• Wash the rice well and place in a bowl.

• In a hot pan, sauté the onion in the oil for 2 minutes.

• Add the diced lamb and the spices and fold together. Remove from the heat.

• Add the meat mixture to the rice and stir to combine.

• Place the cutlets in the base of a saucepan. Top with tomato slices.

• Place a vine leaf on your work surface board with the inside of the leaf facing up, and place about 1 tsp of the rice mix on the leaf.

• Fold the sides of the leaf towards the centre and partially over the filling, and carefully roll from the bottom, tightly, to form a small cigar. Continue making these until all of the mixture is used up.

• Place these on top of the cutlets, fitting them closely together to fill the space, and then layering as necessary, as you go.

• Cover the vine leaves with water. Add the lemon juice. Place a flat plate, roughly the same diameter as the saucepan, on top of the filled vine leaves. Place a weight on the plate to hold the filled vine leaves in place and to prevent them unravelling.

• Cover, heat and simmer gently for about 90 minutes. The dish is ready when the rice is tender.

• Remove the weight, pour off any excess liquid and carefully remove the plate (it will still be hot).

• To serve, carefully upend the saucepan onto a large, flat serving dish.

KEBBEH... *it's in your hands*

This is a wonderfully versatile dish. From the basic recipe, you can make kebbeh balls with their meat filling and fine meat casings, as in the recipe below. Or you can layer it in a baking tray with the filling in the middle. Also, it can be baked or fried. Or the balls can be made larger and cooked on a barbecue. You can even make it vegetarian – with a pumpkin and potato casing and a chickpea filling. In fact, you can be endlessly creative with kebbeh.

INGREDIENTS

500g fine burghul

1½ tsp salt

1½ tsp pepper

1 tsp mixed spice (baharat) 🌴

1 tsp dried mint

3 tbs rice bran oil, and more for frying

100g pine nuts

2 onions, 1 finely chopped

500g minced beef or lamb

500g lamb topside

NOTE: For baked Kebbeh, place one layer of shell mixture in a baking dish and top with a layer of the filling. Then, top this with another layer of shell mixture. Brush with ½ cup rice bran oil, cut into squares or diamonds and bake at 180 C for 40 minutes.

METHOD

kebbeh shell mixture

• In a medium bowl, soak burghul for an hour in 1 cup water; drain off any unabsorbed water.

• Blend lamb topside to a smooth paste in a food processor. Remove and set to one side.

• Process the onion with 1 tsp sea salt and 1 tsp black pepper.

• In a large bowl, combine topside, onion mixture and burghul and knead to a dough-like consistency. (You may need to add a little water to get the desired consistency). Cover and set aside.

kebbeh filling

• In a medium frying pan, sauté the finely chopped onion in 2 tbs rice bran oil.

• Over low heat, add the minced meat and break up with wooden spoon or spatula. Cook for about 30 minutes.

• Add mixed spice, salt, pepper and dried mint.

• In a separate pan, toast the pine nuts over low heat until just golden, about 3 minutes, and add to the meat mixture. Remove from heat and allow to cool.

complete your kebbeh

• Take an egg-sized amount of the shell mixture and form it into a ball. Poke a hole into it to make a space for filling. Add 1tbs of the filling mixture and close the top of the hole to seal the ball by pinching the sides together. You can then shape it to a point, or make it into a football shape, or leave as a ball. You decide.

• Deep-fry your kebbeh in hot oil (180 C), in a saucepan or in a deep fryer for about 10 minutes, or until they are deep brown in colour. Drain on paper towels. (Makes about 24 medium-sized kebbeh.)

vegies to accompany kebbeh

INGREDIENTS

almonds

200g raw almonds, unpeeled

METHOD

• Soak the almonds overnight in 2 cups water.

• Drain just before eating or serving.

INGREDIENTS

carrots

2 carrots

2 lemons

½ tsp sea salt

METHOD

• Peel the carrots, and cut each carrot in quarters, lengthways. Cut each piece into four equal lengths.

• Place these into a serving bowl, top with the juice of the lemons, add the salt, mix well and serve.

RIZ A JEJ... *the sum of its parts*

This classic dish of rice with chicken is another of our family favourites. There was a time in the life of my son George when riz a jej seemed to be the only dish he was prepared to eat. In fact, he ate it so often I am astonished he still enjoys it. Which he does, of course.

INGREDIENTS

1kg skinless chicken breasts

¼ onion

2 cups par-boiled Basmati rice 🌴

1 tsp sea salt

1 tsp "morerockin" seasoning 🌴

1 tsp mixed spice (baharat) 🌴

1 tsp Aleppo pepper

100g slivered almonds

100g pine nuts

3 tbs rice bran oil

METHOD

• Rinse the chicken breasts and place them in a large saucepan. Cover with 2 litres of water. Add the onion, bring to a boil and simmer for 30 minutes.

• Lift the chicken from the liquid and, when it cools sufficiently, tear it into strips. Pour off the liquid and reserve. Rinse and dry the saucepan.

• Warm 1 tbs rice bran oil in the saucepan, add half of the chicken and toss for 2 minutes. Rinse the rice well and add it to the chicken in the saucepan and toss together for 2 more minutes. Add 4 cups of the reserved cooking liquid.

• Add the salt and spices to the saucepan, bring to a boil and simmer for 5 minutes. Cover, take off the heat and set aside for 20 minutes until the water is absorbed.

• Warm the remaining 2 tbs rice bran oil in a hot pan and toast the almonds for 3 minutes. Add the pine nuts and toast for a further 2 minutes.

• Add the rest of the chicken strips to the pan and toss with the nuts for 2 more minutes.

• To assemble, tip the rice and chicken out of the saucepan onto a serving dish. Top with the toasted nuts and chicken and, for a fiery finish, sprinkle Aleppo pepper on top.

DAWOOD BASHA... *meatballs with attitude*

This traditional meatball recipe is a Middle Eastern variation on a universal theme. And this is my interpretation of that variation. You can make the meatballs any size you like and, if you would like them spicier, simply add a pinch or two of cayenne to the meat mixture or to the sauce.

INGREDIENTS

meatballs

1kg lamb mince, lean

½ red capsicum, finely diced

¼ tsp freshly ground black pepper

¼ tsp sweet paprika

¼ tsp ground cardamom

¼ tsp ground cloves

¼ tsp ground nutmeg

sauce

2 onions, roughly chopped

300g tomato paste

400g tin whole tomatoes

1 tsp sea salt

1 tsp freshly ground black pepper

2 tbs rice bran oil

garnish

½ red and ½ green capsicum, seeds and pith removed, lightly roasted and peeled if you prefer, each cut into six pieces.

METHOD

meatballs

• Set an oven to 180 C. Mix the meat, by hand, with the capsicum and the spices. Ensure mixture is well combined.

• Roll into balls of about 3cm in diameter and place on a lightly oiled baking tray.

• Place in the oven and bake for 20 minutes.

sauce

• Gently heat the oil in a large saucepan and sweat the onions for 10 minutes. Add the contents of the can of tomatoes, the tomato paste, the salt, pepper and spices and a litre of water. Bring this mixture to a boil, add the meatballs, return to a boil and simmer for 5 minutes.

to serve

• Transfer to a serving bowl and garnish with the red and green capsicum pieces. Serve with traditional rice (Page 78).

CHICKEN WITH YALLATEEF... *savour the flavour*

The magic of yallateef – the condiment, as well as this book – is the way in which it can add, complement and shape flavours. And there is no better example than this dish in which I use it to add a new dimension to a wholesome and delicate, but sometimes bland and uninteresting cut of meat – skinless chicken breasts. You can, of course, use a similar approach to other cuts of chicken, such as skinless thighs. But try the breasts first and be amazed by the miracle of flavour that emerges.

INGREDIENTS

1kg skinless chicken breasts, washed and cut into bite-sized pieces

1 tbs yallateef 🌴 (Page 5)

½ lemon

½ tsp sea salt

1 tbs rice bran oil

METHOD

• Heat a trustworthy pan and add the oil. Salt the chicken and add to the pan, but be aware the oil is likely to greet the arrival of the cold chicken pieces by spitting at you. It's nothing personal.

• When the chicken pieces are becoming golden on one side (about 4-5 minutes) turn them, and cook the second sides (about 2-3 minutes).

• Add the yallateef to the pan and toss well to coat the chicken.

• Finally, squeeze lemon over the chicken, toss well and remove from the heat.

• Serve on rice, with salad or as mezza.

FISH TAJINE... *go with the flow*

My mother cooked our family meals in an old terracotta pot rested on hot stones over burning charcoal. I learned to wait patiently for my food and, when I discovered tajine cooking later in life, the slowness involved reminded me of those times, and the way my mother would cook miraculous food without any of the "conveniences" we enjoy today. The flavours that develop within a tajine are unlike anything else, and this recipe delivers the best of them.

INGREDIENTS

6 fish fillets (your choice),
each around 200g and cut in half.
I often mix them, and use salmon,
rockling and trevally.

1 carrot, sliced into 2cm lengths

1 tsp charlic 🌴

½ tsp sweet paprika

½ tsp dried turmeric

½ tsp sea salt

½ tsp ras el hanout

½ tsp fish spice 🌴

½ tsp zaatar

½ tsp sumac

½ preserved lemon,
halved again, lengthways

1 tbs fresh coriander, chopped

1 tbs flat-leaf parsley, chopped
(leaves only)

1 tbs yallateef 🌴 (Page 5)

1 tbs spicy garlic dip 🌴

1 tbs rice bran oil

1 tbs hazelnut meal

METHOD

• To prepare the fish, rub rock salt and ras el hanout into the pieces and refrigerate for 3-4 hours. Remove, rinse and set aside to dry.

• Place the tajine base on a stove-top on low and add the oil. When it is warm, add the carrot and the yallateef and cook for 3 minutes.

• Add the coriander and the parsley and combine well.

• Slice the flesh from the rind of both segments of preserved lemon and set the rind aside to slice finely as a garnish; add the flesh to the mixture.

• Add spices, charlic and spicy garlic dip.

• Add 1 cup water, and then the hazelnut meal to thicken.

• Cover, bring to a gentle boil and add the fish. Cover and cook for 15 minutes. Or place the tajine, lid on, in an oven at 160 C for 30 minutes.

• Before serving, garnish with fresh pomegranate seeds, parsley and preserved lemon rind.

garnish

fresh pomegranate seeds or dried barberries

flat-leaf parsley, leaves only

preserved lemon rind, sliced finely

NOTE: If using a tajine for the first time be sure to season it first: soak the top and bottom in water overnight, allow to dry the next day then coat the entire tajine with a thin layer of vegetable oil and place in an oven at 100 C for an hour. You need to do this only once, but always use your tajine over gentle heat.

KAFTA & POTATOES... *a winter winner*

Kafta is strangely addictive. But fortunately, this glorious combination of lamb and parsley is also deliciously simple to prepare. And versatile: you can shape kafta into sausages for the barbecue, or spread it on pita bread for an easy pizza. Here, we combine kafta with potatoes and bake it with tomato puree – thus creating a dish which is especially good served with traditional rice (Page 78) at the dead of winter.

INGREDIENTS

1kg minced lamb (lean)

1 onion, large

½ small onion, sliced into rings and flash-fried in a little rice bran oil

1 bunch flat-leaf parsley, washed and de-stemmed

1 tsp sea salt

½ tsp black pepper

½ tsp kafta spice 🌴

10 leaves fresh mint (chopped) or ½ tsp dried mint

1kg waxy potatoes (desiree are fine), washed, skins on – sliced 1cm thick

1 x 680ml bottle tomato purée (or 700g bottle tomato passata if easier to find)

3 medium tomatoes, sliced

METHOD

• Place the onion in a food processor and process briefly. Add the parsley and continue to process until the mixture is fine. Add the spices.

• Place the mixture in a bowl and add the mince. Combine well with your hands.

• Dip your hands into cold water to prevent the meat sticking, and form the kafta into 3cm balls. Flatten.

• Put the kafta in a baking dish and place in an oven, at 180 C, for 10 to 15 minutes. Remove from the oven, top with the potatoes, then pour the tomato purée and 1 litre water over the top. Top with the sliced tomatoes, onion rings and mint. Cover and return to the oven for 30 minutes.

• Remove and serve with traditional rice (Page 78).

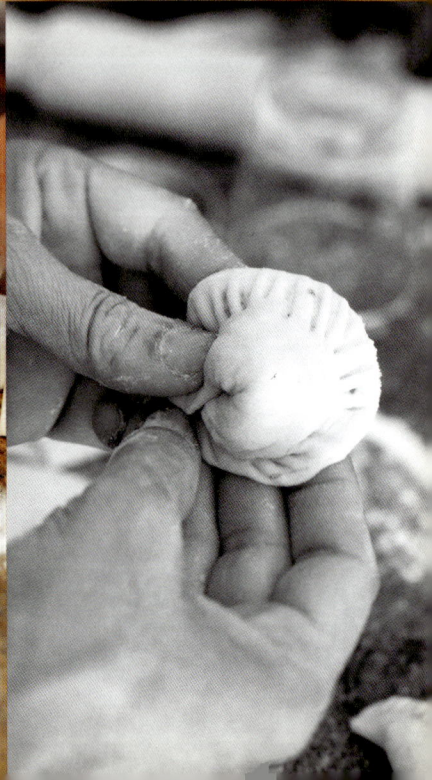

SHISH BARAK... *pass the parcels*

The yoghurt sauce central to this much-loved dish is lighter and tastier than a traditional white sauce, and the lamb parcels soak it up deliciously. You can, however, serve the parcels without the sauce – as finger food. My kids loved to help me roll the dough and cut the pastry discs for this dish. In fact, they loved helping to make their meals almost as much as they loved eating them.

INGREDIENTS

dough

500g plain flour

½ tsp sea salt

filling

2 tsp rice bran oil

500g lamb, minced

1 onion, diced

1 tsp sea salt

1 tsp mixed spice (baharat) 🌴

sauce

1 cup natural yoghurt

1 tsp corn flour

1 tsp sea salt

½ tsp white pepper

2 bay leaves

1 tsp chopped coriander leaves

METHOD

• For the dough, combine the flour, 250ml water and salt into a dough and knead for about 30 minutes. Roll into a ball, cover with plastic wrap and set aside.

• For the filling, heat the oil in a pan. Sauté the onion and, when it has coloured slightly, add the meat and cook for 20 minutes, stirring. Set aside.

• Unwrap the dough on a lightly floured board and roll it out to a thickness of 2mm. Cut out 7-8cm discs with a cutter or rim of a glass. Gather the leftover dough into a ball and roll it out again – cutting more discs. Repeat until all of the dough is used. Cover the discs to prevent them from drying.

• Set an oven to 180 C. Place several of the discs on the floured board and place 1 tsp of the lamb mixture into the centre of each. With your finger, lightly apply water just inside the perimeter of each disc and fold it in half. Using the tines of a fork, lightly press down around the edges to seal each parcel. Repeat until all the discs and/or all of the filling is used up.

• Place finished parcels on a large, lightly-oiled baking tray and brush the tops of each lightly with oil. Bake for 15-20 minutes, or until the tops are golden.

• Place a wide saucepan over low heat and add the yoghurt and 2 cups water, stirring.

• Add the bay leaves and the coriander and continue to stir the mixture as you bring it gently to a boil. Season with salt and pepper and add the corn flour to thicken.

• Take it off the heat and gently ease the parcels into the sauce. Serve in small bowls.

SPICY FISH FILLETS... *saucy seduction*

The tahini in this dish delivers a seductive sauce that enhances the delicate seafood flavours. A range of fish fillets can be used, but I suggest sturdy fillets – salmon, blue-eye, hapuku or trevally. The dish can be served on its own, or on a bed of quinoa rice (Page 102) which will be transformed by the delectable sauce.

INGREDIENTS

fish

1½kg sturdy fish fillets (see above)

½ tsp sea salt

½ tsp sumac

½ tsp Aleppo pepper

1 tbs EV olive oil

1 tsp pomegranate molasses

sauce

500g tahini dip (Page 12)

¼ tsp sea salt

400g yallateef 🌴 (Page 5)

garnish

2 tbs rice bran oil

200g pine nuts

flat-leaf parsley, leaves only, chopped

1 lemon, washed and thinly sliced

METHOD

• Set your oven to 200 C.

• Rinse the fish fillets and coat evenly with the EV olive oil, pomegranate molasses, spices and sea salt. Place on a baking tray and bake for 20 minutes.

• Remove from the oven and set aside to cool.

• Make the sauce: combine the tahini dip, sea salt and 1 cup water in a small saucepan and bring to a boil. Continue to cook over medium heat for 10 minutes. Now, continue to stir the mixture until it thickens – a further 3 minutes. Remove from the heat and fold in the parsley.

• To prepare the pine nuts, fry them, carefully, in a thick-based frying pan for 5 minutes, or until they are golden brown.

• Break the fish fillets into chunks and place half in the bottom of a warm serving dish. Layer with yallateef and top with the rest of the fish. Carefully distribute the hot sauce over the fish and garnish with the pine nuts, more of the parsley and the lemon slices.

MAQLUBA... *deliciously inverted*

Maqluba means upside-down, which makes this inverted rice cake quite a surprise packet. For a vegetarian version simply substitute more eggplant for the meat. And you can build the cake as high as your container will allow, or make the dish as single serves by using small individual containers.

INGREDIENTS

rice

2 cups basmati rice, rinsed well

2 tbs rice bran oil spread (a margarine-like spread made with rice bran oil)

½ tsp sea salt

½ tsp mixed spice (baharat) 🌴

¼ tsp Maras chilli

meat

250g lamb back strap, diced (1cm cubes)

¼ onion, diced

¼ tsp sea salt

½ tsp ras el hanout

½ tsp rice bran oil

eggplant

2 eggplants

1 tsp rice bran oil

½ tsp sea salt

garnish

2 tbs rice bran oil

100g pine nuts

100g blanched almonds, halved

METHOD

• In a large saucepan, melt the rice bran oil spread, add the spices and combine. Add the rice and 4 cups water, bring to a boil and cook for 2 minutes. Turn off the heat and set aside, covered, for 20 minutes until all the water has been absorbed.

• To prepare the meat, add the oil to a hot pan and sauté the onion, meat, salt and spices. Sauté over high heat for 5 minutes and set aside.

• To prepare the eggplant, slice into 1cm discs, rub both sides with salt and oil, pan fry or grill for 5 minutes a side and set aside.

• For the garnish, add the oil to a hot pan and sauté the nuts for 4 minutes. Set aside.

• To assemble, place the nuts on the bottom of a deep, cylindrical container of roughly 20-30cm in diameter and top with a 3cm layer of rice. Press this into place. Then top with a layer of eggplant, and then the meat in a layer. Top this with a second layer of rice. To increase the height of the dish, add an additional layer of rice between the eggplant and the meat.

• Put pressure on the contents of this dish to press the components into place for this next step: place a large, serving plate on top of the container and flip the container.

• Carefully remove the container, leaving the rice-eggplant-meat tower on the serving plate.

CHICKEN MOLOKHIA… *as you like it*

This dish, of Egyptian origin, has become a much-loved standard in the Middle East. It is adored in Lebanon where we eat it as a stew – the form that will result from this recipe. Egyptians, however, are inclined to slice the molokhia leaves very finely and serve the dish as a soup. When we serve our version, we offer an array of extras on the side, and everyone has their own favourite way of eating it: some with extra onion, some with extra lemon, but always with crisp pita bread to soak up the tangy juices.

INGREDIENTS

250g dried molokhia 🌿

1kg skinless chicken breasts, sliced into strips

¼ onion

1 tsp garlic & herbs 🌿

½ tsp crushed black pepper

1 tsp sea salt

1 tbs chopped fresh coriander

1 tsp crushed garlic

1 tsp EV olive oil

2 tbs lemon juice

on the side

onion, finely diced

pita bread (crisped in the oven for 8 minutes at 180 C).

lemon juice

white vinegar

METHOD

• Wash the chicken and place in a large pot. Cover with 2 litres boiling water, add the onion, return to a boil and simmer for 30 minutes. Skim the dish as thoroughly as you can while it is cooking.

• Add the spices, salt, pepper and lemon juice to the chicken.

• Meanwhile, heat the oil in a pan and fry the fresh coriander and the garlic for 3 minutes. Add this mixture to the chicken

• Rinse the molokhia leaves, then add them to the chicken. Return to a boil and simmer for 10 minutes

• Pour the stew into a large bowl, check the seasoning and serve with the side dishes.

NOTE: We usually put a ladle of the stew into a bowl, top with a small handful of the bread and a sprinkle of diced onion, a splash of lemon juice and another of vinegar. But there are no rules! The stew can also be served on traditional rice. (Page 78)

LAMB RIBS & CHICKPEAS… *warm your heart*

Chickpeas, in their own quiet and unassuming way, are a miraculous food: nourishing, versatile and delicious. In this recipe, they cosy up with lamb ribs in a dish which, either served on its own or on a bed of spicy rice (Page 109), will deliver warmth in the chilliest of weather.

INGREDIENTS

2kg lamb ribs

3 onions, peeled and quartered

1kg ripe tomatoes, quartered

½kg washed potatoes, cut into 2cm chunks

500g dried chickpeas, soaked in water overnight

1 tsp sea salt

1 tsp garlic & herbs 🌿

¼ tsp turmeric

¼ tsp ground cumin

1 tsp rice flour

METHOD

• In a large stockpot, bring the ribs and onions to a boil in about 7 litres of water. Simmer for 90 minutes. Lift the ribs and onions from the water, remove as much fat as you can from the ribs and cut them into smaller and more manageable pieces – a minimum of 2 rib bones in each piece. Let them cool, and refrigerate.

• Pour the cooking liquid into a large container, allow to cool and then refrigerate for at least 2 hours. The stock will settle and you will be able to remove and discard the top layer of fat and residue.

• Return the stock, the rib pieces, the onion and the soaked chickpeas to the original stockpot. Bring to a boil over medium heat, and simmer for 30 minutes.

• Add the potatoes and cook for another 20 minutes.

• Add the tomatoes, salt and spices and cook for a further 10 minutes.

• Finally, add the rice flour to thicken the sauce, stirring it in well. Check the seasoning and serve.

SPAGHETTI… *doing it my way*

Numerous surveys of our eating habits have identified spaghetti bolognese – an "Italian" dish with which, curiously, Italians are unfamiliar as they use irregular pasta shapes for meat sauces – as Australia's favourite family dish. So if you like it, try my variation: I was 10 years old when I first cooked this for my younger brother. And it was one of the first recipes I taught my daughter.

INGREDIENTS

pasta and filling

1 x 500g packet spaghetti

500g minced lamb
(or beef, if you prefer)

2 tbs rice bran oil

1 onion, chopped

2 garlic cloves, finely sliced

1 tsp sea salt

½ tsp mixed spice (baharat) 🌴

1 tsp fine black pepper

1 tsp dried mint

1 tsp ras el hanout

sauce

1 cup tomato purée or passata

½ tsp Italian herbs 🌴

½ tsp sea salt

METHOD

• To make the sauce combine a cup of water with the tomato purée or passata, add the salt and herbs and carefully pour into an ovenproof dish or baking dish.

• Bring 3 litres of water to a rolling boil, add the salt and immerse the spaghetti. Cook for 10 minutes. Drain and rinse in cold water to stop it cooking further.

• Pick up clumps of the cooked spaghetti with tongs and form into nests by twisting as you lower the pasta onto an oiled baking sheet. Make six of these nests, and let them cool and set for a minute in the refrigerator.

• Carefully lift the chilled pasta nests, one at a time, with a spatula and position them in the sauce in the ovenproof dish.

• Gently warm oil in a pan, sweat the onion, garlic and spices briefly, add the meat, combine well, add salt to taste and cook for 30 minutes.

• Spoon this mixture into the nests, sharing it evenly.

• Cover the ovenproof dish with foil and bake for 20 mins at 180 C. Remove the foil and bake for a further 5 minutes to crisp the tops.

• Each nest is a serve.

QUAIL MY WAY... *go for goji*

Goji berries are delectable little things, as this dish demonstrates: their gentle sweetness complements the delicacy of tiny quail. This dish is quick and simple, but somehow gives an impression of complexity. Which is what life in the kitchen is all about, really.

INGREDIENTS

6 quail

½ cup basmati rice

100g dried goji berries

50g pine nuts

50g split, blanched almonds

1 tsp rice bran oil

½ tsp sea salt

1 tsp ras el hanout

sauce

1 tsp crushed garlic

1 tsp fresh coriander

1 tsp sea salt

2 lemon

2 pieces preserved lemon flesh

METHOD

• Set an oven to 180 C.

• Rub the quail with lemon and salt, and then wash them.

• Wash the rice thoroughly, add the spices to the drained rice in a bowl and top with a cup of boiling water.

• Cover with plastic wrap and set aside for 20 minutes, until all the water is absorbed. The rice will still be uncooked.

• Add the rice bran oil to a hot pan and toast the nuts with the berries until the nuts colour slightly (2 minutes). Add to the rice.

• Stuff the quail with the rice mixture.

• Combine the sauce ingredients with 2 cups water and pour into a baking dish or a deep baking tray. Add any leftover rice mixture.

• Place the quail in the baking dish and bake for 40 minutes.

• Remove from the oven, carefully lift out the quail and drape with the sauce.

KABSA… *ancient and modern*

This is my version of an ancient meat and rice dish of Yemeni origin that remains hugely popular in the Gulf States of the Middle East where it is also made with goat and even camel. Kabsa is traditionally served on its own, but it's great with a little yoghurt on the side.

INGREDIENTS

5 lamb shanks

1kg skinless chicken breasts

2 cups par-boiled Basmati rice 🌴

100g dried lemon

1 tsp sea salt

1 tsp kabsa spice 🌴

½ tsp garlic & herbs 🌴

½ tsp Maras chilli

½ tsp freshly ground pepper

1 onion, chopped

2 tbs rice bran oil

100g dried barberries

METHOD

• Bring the lamb shanks to a boil in 3 litres of water and simmer for 2 hours, or until the meat is meltingly tender and close to falling off the bone. Lift the shanks from the saucepan and reserve the stock.

• Meanwhile, bring the chicken to a boil in a litre of water and simmer for 30 minutes, skimming as necessary. Lift the chicken from the saucepan, and reserve the stock.

• Combine the chicken and lamb stock and reserve 4 cups of this rich liquid. Discard the remaining stock, or reserve and refrigerate or freeze for a later use.

• Tear the chicken into strips, and also pull the lamb from the bone.

• In a large saucepan, heat the rice bran oil and sauté the onion until it begins to colour. Add the rice, the 4 cups of reserved stock and the dried lemon.

• Fold the lamb and chicken into the rice mixture.

• Add the spices and bring the mixture to a boil. Take off the heat, cover and set aside for 30 minutes, or until the water has been fully absorbed. Fold the barberries through before serving.

NOTE: This recipe delivers a substantial amount of food so, if you don't want to serve it all at once, freeze a proportion of the cooked meat and its stock, and adjust the recipe accordingly. To serve it, defrost and warm the meat in its stock, and return to the recipe from there.

STUFFED VEGETABLES… *core assets*

Choosing vegies from the wonderful array available to us almost all year round can be tricky. So why not serve them all? Or as many of them as you have to hand? Hollowing vegetables can be tedious, but not if you use a zucchini corer, or even a small apple corer, or a melon baller.

INGREDIENTS

2 potatoes, washed

2 large carrots

2 medium capsicums

2 white (Lebanese) zucchini

2 small eggplants

2 red onions

2 brown onions (finely chopped)

½ tsp sea salt

½ tsp cajun spice

½ tsp crushed pepper

½ tsp zaatar

1 garlic clove, finely sliced

1 tbs rice bran oil

200g minced lamb

¼ tsp mixed spice (baharat) 🌿

pinch sea salt

50g pine nuts

500g tomato purée

½ tsp tajine spice 🌿

½ tsp garlic & herbs 🌿

METHOD

• Slice the tops off the potatoes, capsicums, red onions, zucchini and eggplants. Scoop out the insides and discard.

• Cut the carrots in half and scoop out the centre of the thicker half.

• Place the vegetables in a bowl of water to prevent them from discolouring while you prepare the stuffing.

• In a hot pan, sweat the onion and garlic in the oil until translucent – about 3 minutes. Top with the meat, a pinch of salt and the mixed spice. Increase the heat and stir to combine and brown the meat – about 20 minutes. Add the pine nuts and cook for a further 5 minutes.

• Lift the vegetables from the water and drain. Stuff with the meat mixture.

• Mix ½ cup water, tomato purée, tajine spice and the garlic & herbs, and pour into a deep baking tray. Place the vegetables in the purée mixture, cover with foil and place in the oven at 180 C for 40 minutes.

• Remove the foil and return to the oven to brown the tops for 5 minutes.

• Serve each stuffed vegetable with a spoonful of the sauce – perhaps on top of quinoa rice (Page 102).

RICOTTA & JAM CIGARS... *no smoking*

This is our version of an old favourite: znud el sit, which is a filo cigar filled with clotted cream. These ricotta and jam variations are a hit in our cafe: we make them every day, sometimes three times a day. They offer the perfect balance of sweet and savoury, and they are fun.

INGREDIENTS

1 x 375g packet filo pastry

1.2kg ricotta (cheese)

200g jam (your choice)

½ cup orange blossom syrup (Page 155)

rice bran oil (for deep frying)

ground pistachio (to serve)

METHOD

• Take a sheet of filo, ensuring there are two layers, and place flat on a cutting surface. Using a very sharp knife, cut the sheet into rectangles of about 15cm by 23cm.

• Place 2 tbs of ricotta, loosely formed into a rough cylinder, at the centre of the bottom of each sheet, but not stretching right across the sheet. Top with ½ tbs of jam.

• Fold in the sides of the filo – over the ricotta and the jam – and then roll the sheet, from the bottom, into a cigar shape. As you approach the end of the sheet, wipe a wet finger across the end of the filo to glue the cigar closed, and to prevent it coming apart when you fry it.

• Continue this process until either the filling or the filo – or both – are finished. This recipe should make about 20 cigars.

• Heat a suitable depth of rice bran oil in either a deep-fryer or a saucepan to a temperature of close to 180 C, and deep fry the cigars for about six minutes, in which time they should become golden.

• Lift from the oil with a slotted spoon onto a non-stick baking tray and drizzle with the syrup while they are still hot.

• Serve with ground pistachios, or with more syrup if you would like them to be sweeter.

NOTE: You can make the cigars well in advance, and keep them in the fridge until you are ready to deep-fry them.

POMACHIO YOGHURT...*simple sweetness*

When I crave something sweet, I turn to this simple and nutritious solution. It's a dish you can build upon with whatever you have to hand. Start with the vanilla yoghurt and the pomegranate molasses or syrup, and expand from there by adding fruit (fresh or dried), oats, nuts or even chocolate: the choice (and the pleasure) is yours.

INGREDIENTS

vanilla yoghurt

slivered pistachios

pomegranate molasses or pomegranate syrup (grenadine)

pomegranate seeds

Archie's blend 🌴

METHOD

• Place a couple of drops of the pomegranate syrup or molasses in the inside of a small cup, sprinkle a layer of Archie's blend into the bottom of the cup and fill it, to about ¾, with yoghurt.

• Top with another dollop of pomegranate molasses or syrup and sprinkle with pistachios and pomegranate seeds.

NANA'S TEA... *for whatever ails you*

One winter, the family came down with heavy colds. My daughter, in desperation, made this tea. It worked, helping us make it through a challenging week. And now, whenever one of us is not at the top of our game, we turn to the tea. And even when I'm at my best, I drink it. In fact, I'm drinking it right now...

INGREDIENTS

1 tsp dried hibiscus

1 tsp dried chamomile

1 tsp dried lemongrass

½ tsp aniseed (seeds)

1 tsp dried ginger

1 tsp honey (generous)

15ml fresh lemon juice

½ tsp dried mint

1 cinnamon stick

METHOD

• Place the ingredients in a medium to large teapot. Add 500ml boiling water and allow to infuse for 3 minutes.

• Adjust the tea to your own taste. If it is too strong, add boiling water. And if you prefer it sweeter, add more honey.

• You can reuse the drained, dried ingredients, simply by adding more lemon and honey.

FLOURLESS ALMOND BISCOTTI… *classy nibbles*

These tasty little treasures are a family favourite, and hugely popular in our cafe. They're user-friendly: soft, and not especially sweet. And there's nothing better with coffee – whether they are finished by rolling them in flaked almonds, pistachios, sesame seeds or even chocolate. Surprise yourself!

INGREDIENTS

4 egg whites

2 cups caster sugar

½ tsp vanilla extract

5½ cups almond meal

100g flaked almonds

icing sugar

METHOD

• Set an oven to 180 C. Place the egg whites in a food processor and process until creamy.

• Add the caster sugar, vanilla essence and almond meal, processing after adding each ingredient.

• Once the mixture forms an even dough, roll into the desired shapes.

• Roll the shapes in almond flakes, and place on a non-stick baking tray, or on baking parchment on a regular tray.

• Place in the oven for 15 minutes or until just a hint of golden colour appears on top of each biscotti. Remove from the oven and allow to set for 5 minutes.

• Remove from the tray to a cooling rack and sprinkle with icing sugar. Let them cool before serving. They will keep in an airtight container for up to two weeks. But only if no one knows they're there!

COCONUT CAKE… *moist beyond measure*

As luck would have it, I was introduced to this wonderful cake by my mother-in-law, Saide, who taught me how to make it. The syrup it absorbs makes this cake gloriously moist and indulgent – and entirely irresistible.

INGREDIENTS

2 cups fine desiccated coconut

1 cup self-raising flour

1 cup whole milk

1 cup caster sugar

2 eggs

1 tsp baking powder

1 tsp vanilla extract

100g raw almonds, unpeeled

1 tbs rice bran oil

2 cups orange blossom syrup (Page 155)

METHOD

• Heat an oven to 180 C. In a large bowl – ideally on a food-mixer – beat the eggs and caster sugar until light and creamy.

• Add the coconut, flour, baking powder and vanilla extract and combine well. Then add the milk and mix vigorously.

• Oil a 30cm by 25cm baking tray with 5cm high sides, ensuring the corners and sides are coated. Pour the mixture into the baking tray.

• Slice into 5cm squares.

• In the centre of each square place one almond.

• Place the tray in the oven and cook for 40 minutes.

• Remove the tray from the oven and re-cut the squares. Then carefully pour the syrup evenly over the entire cake.

• Return it to the oven and bake for a further 2 minutes to allow the cake to absorb the syrup. Allow to cool before serving.

ORANGE BLOSSOM SYRUP… *sweet mystery*

This seductive syrup adds a finishing touch to many sweets, including ricotta and jam cigars, kuneffa and Lebanese donuts.

INGREDIENTS

2 cups caster sugar

1 tsp orange blossom water

squeeze lemon juice or pinch citric acid

METHOD

• Heat the sugar with 1 cup water and the lemon juice or citric acid in a saucepan until dissolved. Bring to a boil and simmer for 5 minutes.

• Take off the heat, add the orange blossom water and stir.

• Allow to cool before using.

CRANBERRY PUDDING… *a fruit 'n' nut case*

This creation came about because so many puddings are, for me anyway, far too sweet. This one, however, lets you decide just how sweet you want it to be: it all depends upon how much syrup you ladle into each serving at the end.

INGREDIENTS

pudding

3 cups full cream milk

½ cup cream

2 tbs coarse semolina

2 tbs rice flour

2 tsp sugar

½ tsp orange blossom water

garnish

pomegranate syrup (grenadine)

ground pistachio

1 tbs orange blossom syrup (Page 155)

cranberry mixture

50g dried cranberries

½ tsp caster sugar

METHOD

• Warm the milk in a large saucepan. Add the cream, semolina and rice flour. Keep stirring over gentle to medium heat until the mixture comes to a boil and thickens.

• Remove from the heat. Add the sugar and orange blossom water and stir for 2 minutes to dissolve the sugar and even out the pudding.

• Place a few drops of pomegranate syrup into a mid-sized drinking glass, to one side, and swirl the glass. Immediately pour the mixture into the glass to within 1cm of the top. Continue to fill glasses in this way until the mixture is used up. Allow to cool for an hour.

• Place 1 tsp of the cranberry mixture – made by combining the dried cranberries with the orange blossom syrup, gently bringing to a boil and then allowing to cool – in the centre of the surface of the pudding, and sprinkle pistachios around the edges. Top with orange blossom syrup to taste, and serve.

NOTE: Cover each filled glass with cling wrap and this pudding will keep, in the refrigerator, for up to a week.

SESAME & ANISEED BISCUITS... *bring a tin*

Whenever I visit my mother-in-law, she will produce, as if by magic, a tin of these delectable biscuits. We will sit in her kitchen endlessly talking, laughing and sometimes making even more of these biscuits – enough for the whole family. I also make this sugar-free version for our cafe using Xylitol, a natural sweetener.

INGREDIENTS

1kg self-raising flour

1 cup whole milk

1 cup EV olive oil

1 cup Xylitol

4 whole eggs

1 tbs aniseed (seeds)

1 cup raw sesame seeds

METHOD

• Set an oven to 180 C. Cream the eggs and Xylitol in a food mixer and, with the motor still running, add the oil and mix well.

• Add the flour and the aniseed, and then the milk. Mix to a firm dough.

• Roll into small "snakes" of about 12cm in length and 1cm thick, then join the ends to form circles.

• Roll in the sesame seeds, allowing them to adhere to the outsides. Place on a non-stick baking tray and bake for 40 minutes, or until they become golden.

LEBANESE COFFEE... *sweet and strong*

If you like your coffee strong, you will love this coffee, but you can always adjust it to your own preference. We are inclined to drink it black and in demitasse cups, but the decisions you are faced with are: (a) how sweet would you like it? and (b) would you like cardamom added? Try (a) very! and (b) yes, please!

INGREDIENTS

2 tsp ground Lebanese coffee

pinch ground cardamom (optional)

1 tsp sugar (optional)

METHOD

• Boil a cup of water in a Lebanese coffee pot; remove from the heat, add the coffee, sugar and cardamom (if using). Stir very well.

• Return to a low heat, stirring only the top half of the coffee. Allow to reach a rolling boil – the point at which the crema will roll over on itself – a minimum of 3 times. Take care during this process as it can overflow quickly if you look away.

• Remove from the heat and before serving allow it to stand for a few minutes to ensure the grounds settle to the base of the pot before pouring.

RIZ BI HALEB... *rice, milk and memories*

This dish – literally rice with milk – has the Proustian ability to transport me back to my childhood: its purity reminds me of simpler times. The mosquito geranium plant can be difficult to find, but the recipe works without it. I spent years in search of the distinctive flavour it imposes on the dish because I had no idea what the plant was called in English, and I stumbled upon it one day when I was out walking. I was given a cutting, planted it behind the shop and, to this day, it is the only plant I grow there.

INGREDIENTS

1 litre whole milk

1 cup rice (short grain)

1 cup caster sugar

1 tsp orange blossom water

1 tsp rose water

3 stems mosquito geranium, tied together

garnish

pistachios, crushed

dried rose petals

cinnamon

METHOD

• Bring 3 cups water to a simmer in a large saucepan. Rinse the rice well and add it to the saucepan. Return to a boil and simmer for about 20 minutes, stirring occasionally.

• Add the milk to the mixture and return to a boil. Simmer for 5 more minutes.

• Add the mosquito geranium and simmer for 2 more minutes. Then remove it from the mixture and discard. Simmer for 5 more minutes, and the mixture will begin to thicken.

• Stirring continuously, add the sugar, orange blossom water and rose water, stirring for another minute before taking it off the heat.

• Pour it, while hot, into bowls or mugs. Allow it to cool in the refrigerator and serve it cold. Covered with cling wrap, it will keep in the fridge for a week. Or serve it hot if you prefer. Either way, garnish with cinnamon, pistachios and rose petals.

LEBANESE DONUTS... *holier than most*

In Lebanon, these gems are part of the traditional celebration of Ghtas, Christ's baptismal night. But at Oasis, these light, crisp, golden jewels are on offer every day. And yes, take care: they are seriously addictive!

INGREDIENTS

500g plain flour

1 tsp sea salt

2 tsp caster sugar

1 tsp rice bran oil

2 tsp dried yeast

rice bran oil for deep-frying

500g orange blossom syrup (Page 155)

METHOD

• Dissolve the yeast in a cup of warm water.

• In a large bowl, combine the flour, sugar, salt, oil and the yeast mixture. Mix well to form a smooth dough.

• In a large, deep pan – a sauté pan close to 10cm in depth is ideal – bring oil, to a depth of about 5cm in the pan, up to a deep-frying temperature of about 180 C.

• Pour the syrup into a bowl and position close to the stovetop.

• Using a long-handled tablespoon, carefully ease portions of the dough – each of roughly 1tbs in volume – into the oil. The first few will scorch, so discard them. But continue, and they will cook to perfection. Be sure to dip the tablespoon into a cup of oil between each use to prevent the batter from sticking.

• Carefully turn the donuts in the oil so they cook evenly on all sides. Then, lift them from the oil with a slotted spoon and, while they are still hot, place them in the syrup. Ensure they remain immersed for a minute, at which point you can lift them out with the slotted spoon, allowing the syrup to drip back into the bowl. Place them on a large, non-stick tray in a single layer.

• When you have finished cooking all of the batter, set the donuts aside to cool before serving. They are best eaten on the day they are made.

NOTE: You will have leftover syrup: strain it, place in a sealed container and reuse for your next batch of donuts. Which you may embark upon just as soon as you have eaten the first batch!

KUNEFFA... *sweet with a crunch*

Eat kuneffa fresh from the oven: you will never forget it. Traditionally, it is made on a base of semolina mixture in large, round trays. In my recipe, however, I use kataifi – a shredded pastry which adds crispness. When I was growing up kuneffa was not a dish made at home. Rather, we bought it from sweet shops. Often.

INGREDIENTS

250g dry kataifi

3 tbs rice bran oil

500g sweet cheese, shredded 🌴
(or use haloumi soaked for 48 hours, changing the water twice, to reduce saltiness)

1 litre whole milk

5 tbs fine semolina

½ cup caster sugar

orange blossom syrup (Page 155)

ground pistachios (to serve)

METHOD

• Heat an oven to 180 C. Add the oil to the kataifi and mix well.

• Evenly spread half the kataifi on the base of a well-oiled, round oven tray of about 30cm in diameter. Set aside the other half.

• Spread the cheese on top of the kataifi.

• In a saucepan, warm the milk. Add the sugar and gradually work in the semolina, stirring until the mixture thickens.

• Carefully pour this mixture over the cheese and cover with the rest of the kataifi.

• Place in the oven for 30 minutes, or until golden.

• Serve with a drizzle of orange blossom syrup and a sprinkle of pistachios – cut into eight servings, as you would a pizza.

INDEX

🌴 Denotes ingredients available only at Oasis.

Yallateef!

Conceived by Oasis Bakery and produced by Hartbeat Media
Title, text, design and concept: © Oasis Bakery/Hartbeat Media 2013
Photographs: © Dean Cambray 2013
First published September 2013.
All rights reserved

National Library of Australia Cataloguing-in-Publication entry
Makool, Marwa.
Yallateef! : Marwa Makool ; Bob Hart; Dean Cambray.
ISBN: 978-0-646-59515-3 (pbk.)
Subjects: Cookery, Lebanese.
Other Authors/Contributors: Makool, Marwa; Cambray, Dean;
Hart, Bob.
Dewey number: 641.5956

Printed in China by The Australian Book Connection

Distributed in Australia by Peribo Pty Limited,
Ph: (02) 9457 0011 or info@peribo.com.au

Foreword: Bob Hart
Food preparation and recipes: Marwa Makool
Photography and styling: Dean Cambray
Design: Dot Alcaide
Editing: Richard Conrad
Production: Keith Downes
Project co-ordination: Natalie Makool

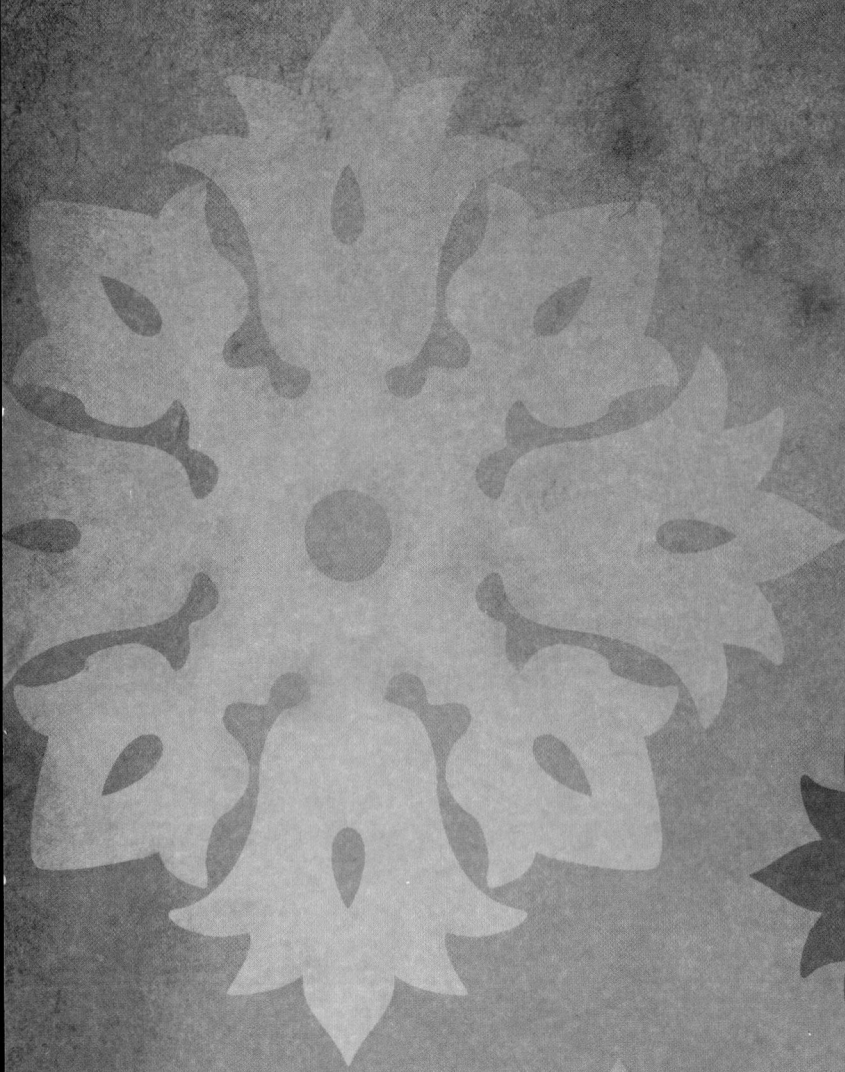